Governance Stability

How to Maintain Control, Prevent Drift, and Adapt Over Time

Mark Ellison

PERENNIAL PUBLISHING

Published by Perennial Publishing

First Edition

Paperback ISBN: 978-1-971996-33-2
Hardcover ISBN: 978-1-971996-34-9
EBook ISBN: 978-1-971996-35-6

For bulk or institutional orders, contact Perennial Publishing.

Contents

Stability Requires Active Governance

The Governance Requirement Mechanism defines a structural condition: financial systems require continuous oversight to maintain stability over time. Stability is not preserved by initial configuration alone. It is not embedded permanently at the point of construction. A system may be well-formed, aligned, and appropriately configured at inception, but this state does not sustain itself without intervention. The mechanism establishes that governance is not an optional layer applied under stress or uncertainty. It is a continuous structural requirement that exists regardless of whether instability is immediately visible.

This requirement emerges from how systems behave over time. Financial systems are composed of interacting elements—income flows, expense loads, liquidity reserves, exposure distributions, and decision processes—that do not remain static. Each component evolves independently and in interaction with others. These changes are not synchronized. They do not occur in coordinated intervals or under centralized control. As a result, the system's configuration begins to shift from its original state the moment it is set in motion. The Governance Requirement Mechanism exists because this shift is constant and directionally uncorrected without active oversight.

The mechanism does not define governance as a set of actions or interventions. It defines governance as a structural function: the process through which the system is observed, evaluated, and adjusted to maintain alignment. Without this function, the system operates passively. Passive operation implies that all changes—whether internal or external—are absorbed without evaluation or correction. Over time, this leads to divergence between the system's current state and the conditions required for stability.

The operation of the Governance Requirement Mechanism begins with the recognition that deviation is continuous. Financial systems do not fail primarily through isolated disruptions. They degrade through accumulated misalignment. Small deviations—changes in expense structure, variation in income timing, shifts in liquidity levels, incremental increases in fixed obligations—do not immediately produce instability. Each change appears manageable in isolation. Each deviation is often below the threshold of immediate consequence. However, the system does not evaluate deviations individually. It reflects their cumulative effect.

In the absence of governance, these deviations compound. The system does not contain an internal corrective force that restores alignment automatically. There is no self-regulating mechanism that returns the system to its prior configuration once it has shifted. Instead, the system continues to operate under the new conditions created by each deviation. This produces gradual drift.

Drift is not a discrete event. It is a directional process. It represents the movement of the system away from its aligned state without a corresponding adjustment. Because drift occurs incrementally, it does not produce immediate feedback. The system continues to function. Obligations are met. Income is received. Expenses are paid. This continuity masks the underlying change. The absence of immediate failure creates the appearance of stability, even as the system's configuration becomes increasingly misaligned.

The Governance Requirement Mechanism operates by interrupting this passive progression. It introduces an active process that observes system behavior, interprets deviations, and initiates adjustment. Monitoring is the first function within this process. Monitoring does not mean observation at arbitrary intervals. It implies continuous awareness of system position relative to stability conditions. This includes tracking the relationship between capacity and load, the distribution of exposures, and the integrity of liquidity buffers. Monitoring establishes visibility. Without visibility, deviation remains undetected until it reaches a level that produces observable consequences.

However, monitoring alone does not maintain stability. Detection without interpretation does not alter system behavior. The second function of governance is feedback interpretation. Feedback is generated by the system continuously. Variations in timing, changes in margins, and shifts in resource availability all produce signals. These signals must be evaluated in relation to system stability. Interpretation determines whether a deviation is neutral, self-correcting, or destabilizing. Without interpretation, all signals are treated equally, and the system cannot distinguish between benign fluctuation and structural degradation.

Once deviation is detected and interpreted, the mechanism proceeds to adjustment. Adjustment is not reactive correction in response to failure. It is the process of recalibrating system components to maintain alignment before instability occurs. This may involve modifying the relationship between capacity and load, redistributing exposure, or reinforcing liquidity layers. The specific form of adjustment is not defined by the mechanism. What is defined is the necessity of adjustment as a continuous process. Without recalibration, the system retains the effects of accumulated deviation.

Constraint enforcement completes the operational cycle. Adjustment alone does not prevent future drift if the conditions that produced the deviation remain unchanged. Constraints define the boundaries within which the system can operate without generating destabilizing deviation. Enforcement ensures that system behavior remains within these boundaries over time. Without constraint enforcement, adjustments are temporary. The system returns to the same patterns that produced misalignment, and drift resumes.

These functions—monitoring, interpretation, adjustment, and constraint enforcement—do not operate sequentially as isolated stages. They form a continuous loop. The system is observed, evaluated, adjusted, and regulated in an ongoing process. The Governance Requirement Mechanism exists within this loop. It is not activated under specific conditions. It is continuously active because the forces that produce deviation are continuously active.

This mechanism interacts with other system components by operating at a different level. Decisions occur within the system. They determine how resources are allocated, how obligations are structured, and how exposures are taken on or reduced. Each decision modifies the system's configuration. However, decisions are localized. They are made at specific points in time, often in response to immediate conditions. Governance operates on the system as a whole. It evaluates the cumulative effect of decisions over time and determines whether the resulting configuration remains aligned with stability requirements.

This distinction is critical. Decisions can be individually correct based on available information and immediate objectives, yet collectively produce misalignment. A decision to increase fixed obligations may be supported by current income levels. A decision to reduce liquidity may be justified by perceived opportunity cost. A decision to concentrate exposure may be aligned with expected outcomes. Each decision can be internally consistent. However, governance evaluates the aggregate effect of these decisions. It determines whether the resulting configuration increases rigidity, reduces margin, or concentrates risk in a way that compromises stability.

Without governance, there is no mechanism to perform this evaluation. The system becomes a collection of decisions without a unifying control layer. Each decision is executed, but their interactions are not assessed. This creates a structural gap. The system lacks the ability to detect when the combined effect of decisions has moved it outside stable operating conditions. The Governance Requirement Mechanism fills this gap by providing a continuous evaluative layer that operates independently of individual decision processes.

The implication for stability is direct. Stability is not a fixed condition that can be achieved and then assumed to persist. It is a maintained state that depends on continuous alignment between system components. Alignment is not static. It must be recalibrated as conditions change. The absence of governance removes the process through which this recalibration occurs. As a result, the system begins to diverge from its stability conditions, even if no single change appears significant.

This divergence is initially invisible. The system continues to function because the margin between current state and failure point has not yet been exhausted. However, stability is defined by this margin. As drift accumulates, the margin narrows. The system becomes more sensitive to disturbance. Variability that would have been absorbed under prior conditions begins to produce stress. Timing mismatches that were previously manageable begin to create pressure. The system's tolerance for disruption decreases.

Importantly, this process does not require incorrect decisions or external shocks. It is driven by the absence of governance. Even in stable external conditions, and even when decisions are internally consistent, the system degrades if it is not actively maintained. This establishes a critical distinction. Instability is not solely the result of adverse events or poor judgment. It is the natural outcome of passive system operation over time.

The failure mode defined by the Governance Requirement Mechanism is therefore not sudden collapse. It is gradual degradation leading to eventual instability. Passive operation allows drift to accumulate without correction. Because drift does not produce immediate consequences, it remains unaddressed. The system adapts to its changing configuration without recognizing the loss of alignment. By the time instability becomes visible, the system has already moved significantly away from its stable state.

At this stage, correction becomes more difficult. The adjustments required to restore alignment are larger. They may involve reversing multiple layers of accumulated deviation. The system may also have reduced flexibility due to increased rigidity or diminished liquidity. This constrains the ability to implement corrective changes. The absence of early governance intervention transforms manageable deviations into structural problems.

The Governance Requirement Mechanism therefore defines both the necessity and the timing of governance. It must be continuous because deviation is continuous. It must be proactive because reactive correction occurs after margin has been reduced. Governance is not a response to instability. It is the process that prevents instability from developing.

This does not imply that governance eliminates all variability or prevents all forms of disturbance. Financial systems remain subject to uncertainty and external change. What governance provides is alignment. It ensures that the system maintains sufficient margin, appropriate distribution of load, and adequate buffering capacity to absorb variation without transitioning into instability. Without this alignment, the same level of external disturbance produces greater impact.

The mechanism also clarifies that governance is not equivalent to increased complexity or constant intervention. It is defined by function, not intensity. Effective governance does not require continuous modification of system components. It requires continuous evaluation and the capacity to adjust when necessary. In the absence of deviation, governance maintains the existing configuration. When deviation is detected, governance initiates recalibration. The process is conditional, but the requirement for the process is constant.

By establishing governance as a structural requirement, the mechanism reframes stability as an active condition. Stability is not the absence of visible problems. It is the presence of continuous alignment. This alignment is not self-sustaining. It is maintained through the ongoing operation of governance processes that monitor, interpret, adjust, and enforce constraints.

The absence of these processes does not produce immediate failure. It produces drift. Drift reduces margin. Reduced margin increases sensitivity. Increased sensitivity converts normal variation into destabilizing pressure. This sequence unfolds gradually, without clear boundaries between stable and unstable states. The system crosses thresholds not through discrete events, but through cumulative change.

The Governance Requirement Mechanism defines this progression and the means by which it is interrupted. By maintaining continuous oversight and adjustment, governance prevents the accumulation of uncorrected deviation. It preserves alignment and sustains the conditions under which the system can absorb variability without loss of stability.

Stability, therefore, is not a condition that persists by default. It is a condition that must be maintained.

The Stability Decay Mechanism

The Stability Decay Mechanism defines the structural tendency for financial systems to lose alignment over time in the absence of active governance. Stability is not a persistent state embedded within the system once it is achieved. It is a temporary condition that exists only while the relationships between system components remain within the bounds required for stable operation. These relationships are not fixed. They are continuously altered by the independent movement of the components that constitute the system. As a result, alignment is not preserved by default. It is gradually eroded as the system evolves.

At any given point, a financial system can be configured such that its components are appropriately balanced. Income may provide sufficient and timely capacity. Expenses may remain within manageable limits relative to that capacity. Liquidity may offer adequate temporal coverage, allowing the system to absorb variation in inflow and outflow. Exposure may be distributed within tolerable ranges, preventing disproportionate impact from localized disruption. This configuration defines a state of alignment. However, the Stability Decay Mechanism establishes that this state is not self-maintaining. It persists only as long as the relationships between these components remain intact, and those relationships are continuously subject to change.

The mechanism operates through the independent and unsynchronized movement of system components. Income does not remain constant in timing, magnitude, or reliability. It fluctuates, introducing variation into the system's capacity profile. Expenses do not remain fixed in structure or baseline. They shift through incremental increases, variability, and the introduction or persistence of obligations. Liquidity is not static. It expands and contracts in response to inflows, outflows, and allocation decisions, altering the system's ability to convert resources into time. Exposure evolves through accumulation, concentration, or redistribution, changing the system's sensitivity to adverse conditions.

These movements occur continuously and without coordination. There is no inherent mechanism within the system that synchronizes changes across components to preserve alignment. Each component adjusts based on its own inputs and conditions. The result is a series of incremental deviations from the system's initial configuration. These deviations are not inherently destabilizing at low levels. The system is capable of absorbing small changes without loss of function. This capacity to absorb variation delays the emergence of observable consequences.

Because small deviations do not produce immediate instability, they are incorporated into the system's operating baseline. The system continues to function, and its current configuration becomes normalized. There is no automatic process that reverses these changes or restores the system to its prior state. Each adjustment persists and becomes the foundation for subsequent changes. The Stability Decay Mechanism is therefore driven by accumulation without correction. Deviation compounds over time because it is neither identified nor counteracted by default.

The absence of immediate feedback is central to the mechanism's operation. Financial systems do not signal misalignment at the point of initial deviation. The system continues to meet obligations and maintain operational continuity. This continuity creates the appearance of stability, even as the underlying configuration shifts. The lack of visible disruption prevents the recognition of decay in its early stages. As a result, the system adapts to its evolving structure without identifying the gradual loss of alignment.

The cumulative effect of these uncorrected deviations is a progressive alteration of the relationships that define stability. Capacity relative to load may decline as expenses increase or income becomes more variable. Liquidity relative to obligation may narrow, reducing the system's temporal buffer. Exposure may become more concentrated, increasing sensitivity to disruption. Each of these changes modifies the system's tolerance for variation. The system remains functional, but its margin for absorbing additional change is reduced.

The mechanism is not dependent on the presence of incorrect decisions. Individual decisions may be internally consistent and appropriate within their immediate context. Adjustments to expenses may reflect current priorities. Changes in liquidity may be influenced by allocation preferences. Shifts in exposure may align with expected outcomes. Each decision may be rational when evaluated in isolation. However, decisions are localized actions. They modify specific components without evaluating the cumulative effect of multiple changes across the system.

The Stability Decay Mechanism operates at the level of aggregation. It reflects the combined impact of numerous small adjustments that are not coordinated to preserve overall alignment. A sequence of individually coherent decisions can produce collective misalignment if their interactions are not continuously evaluated. The mechanism therefore distinguishes between decision quality and system alignment. Decay does not require incorrect decisions. It requires uncoordinated change.

This distinction clarifies the relationship between structure and control. Structure defines how the system is configured at a given point in time. It determines the arrangement and relationships of components. Control defines the processes that maintain or adjust this configuration as conditions evolve. A system may possess a structurally sound configuration at inception, but without control, that configuration will not persist. The Stability Decay Mechanism operates independently of initial system quality because it is driven by ongoing change rather than starting conditions.

A well-structured system does not resist decay through its design alone. The same processes that allow the system to function—continuous flows, adjustments, and interactions—also generate deviation. Without an active process to evaluate and correct these deviations, the system's configuration shifts over time. Structure establishes the initial state. It does not determine the trajectory. The trajectory is defined by whether changes are monitored and adjusted or allowed to accumulate without correction.

The implication for stability is that it cannot be preserved through initial configuration alone. Stability depends on maintaining alignment between components as they evolve. Because these components change continuously, alignment must also be maintained continuously. Passive operation, in which the system is allowed to evolve without oversight, results in progressive misalignment. The concept of "set and forget" assumes that stability is static. The Stability Decay Mechanism demonstrates that stability is dynamic and requires ongoing maintenance.

The temporal progression of the mechanism clarifies how decay develops over time. This progression is not defined by discrete thresholds but by stages characterized by changes in system behavior as alignment erodes.

In the early stage, deviations are small and widely distributed across system components. Income may fluctuate slightly in timing or magnitude. Expenses may increase incrementally or vary within a limited range. Liquidity may decline modestly relative to usage. Exposure may become marginally more concentrated. Each of these changes remains within the system's existing capacity to absorb variation. The system continues to function without interruption. Obligations are met, and variability is contained within available margins. There is no visible indication of instability. Alignment is beginning to erode, but this erosion does not produce feedback that would prompt recognition or response.

Stability appears intact because the system retains sufficient capacity to absorb these changes.

In the mid stage, the accumulation of deviations begins to compress the system's margin. The distance between capacity and load decreases as expenses rise or income becomes less predictable. Liquidity buffers narrow relative to the demands placed on them, reducing the system's temporal flexibility. Variability in income timing produces intermittent pressure that is no longer fully absorbed. Exposure becomes more concentrated, increasing the system's sensitivity to adverse conditions. The system remains operational, but its tolerance for variation is reduced. Fluctuations that were previously neutral begin to produce measurable stress. This stress may appear as tighter timing between inflows and outflows, reduced buffer capacity, or increased reliance on specific sources of income or exposure. The defining characteristic of this stage is margin compression. The system operates closer to its limits, and its ability to absorb additional deviation is diminished.

In the late stage, the system reaches a point where normal variability produces disproportionate impact. The margin that previously absorbed fluctuations has been sufficiently reduced that routine changes generate instability. Income variability that was previously manageable leads to sustained pressure on capacity. Liquidity constraints limit the system's ability to absorb timing mismatches or unexpected demands. Concentrated exposure amplifies the effect of adverse conditions, increasing the impact of disruption. The system transitions from absorbing variability to transmitting it as stress. Instability emerges not as the result of a single event, but as the cumulative outcome of prolonged decay. The system's configuration no longer supports stable operation under normal conditions. Variability that was once contained now propagates through the system, producing constraint and potential failure.

This progression demonstrates that decay is a continuous process that evolves from low visibility to increasing constraint and ultimately to instability. Each stage introduces a distinct change in system behavior. The early stage is defined by absorption without consequence. The mid stage is characterized by reduced tolerance and the emergence of pressure. The late stage is marked by the conversion of normal variability into instability. These stages are connected by the accumulation of uncorrected deviation across system components.

The boundary condition of the Stability Decay Mechanism is passive system operation without governance. In this condition, there is no process to monitor deviations, interpret their significance, or adjust the system to maintain alignment. Changes occur and persist without evaluation. The system continues to function, but its configuration progressively diverges from the conditions required for stability.

Failure under this mechanism is not a discrete event triggered by a singular disruption. It is the result of accumulated decay. Instability emerges when the system's reduced margin is insufficient to absorb normal variability. The transition from stability to instability reflects the cumulative effect of uncorrected deviation rather than the impact of isolated events. The system does not fail because of a single change. It fails because multiple changes have been allowed to accumulate without correction, altering the relationships that define stability.

The Stability Decay Mechanism establishes that decay is the default trajectory of financial systems in the absence of control. Stability is not self-sustaining. It exists only while alignment is maintained, and alignment degrades continuously as components evolve. Without an active process to counteract this degradation, the system moves progressively away from its initial configuration.

This progression begins with small changes that are absorbed without consequence. It continues through the compression of margin and increased sensitivity to variation. It culminates in a state where normal fluctuations produce instability. Each stage reflects the cumulative impact of uncorrected deviation across system components. The mechanism does not depend on external shocks or incorrect decisions. It depends on the absence of a process that maintains alignment over time.

Stability decay begins with small changes that go uncorrected, establishing the foundation for understanding how drift develops within financial systems.

[illegible]

The Drift Mechanism

The Drift Mechanism defines the process through which small, continuous deviations accumulate over time into structural misalignment. Drift is not a discrete break in system behavior. It is not a sudden departure from stable operation, and it does not begin at the point where instability becomes visible. It begins earlier, at the point where alignment starts to move directionally away from the conditions required for stable operation without producing immediate failure. The defining feature of drift is therefore not disruption, but gradual movement. A financial system can continue to function while it is drifting. It can remain operational while its internal relationships become less aligned, less tolerant, and less stable.

This distinction matters because systems are often interpreted through visible outcomes. Stability is inferred from continuity, and instability is inferred from interruption. Drift exists between those two observations. It describes the period in which the system still appears to function normally even though its configuration is changing in a direction that reduces stability. The mechanism establishes that continuity of operation is not evidence of preserved alignment. A system can remain intact at the surface while its structural position deteriorates beneath that continuity.

Drift emerges because system components do not remain fixed once a financial system is established. Income timing changes. Expenses vary in amount, sequence, and baseline. Liquidity rises or falls relative to demand. Exposure shifts through concentration, persistence, or redistribution. These changes are often small when they occur. They do not necessarily exceed tolerance thresholds individually. The system absorbs them. But absorption is not correction. When a deviation is absorbed without adjustment, it becomes part of the system's new operating position. Drift is the cumulative result of this process.

The mechanism operates through accumulation without immediate consequence. A minor change in income timing may not create pressure if liquidity remains sufficient. A modest increase in recurring expense may not create instability if capacity remains above load. A small reduction in liquidity may not matter if variability remains contained. A slight increase in exposure concentration may not produce visible stress while conditions remain favorable. Each change is individually tolerable. The system continues to operate, and because it continues to operate, the change is treated as normal. The baseline shifts.

This shift in baseline is central to the Drift Mechanism. Drift is not simply the presence of deviation. It is the incorporation of deviation into normal system operation. Once a change is absorbed without correction, the system no longer treats it as temporary. It becomes embedded in the operating structure from which future variation is managed. When another small deviation occurs, it is absorbed from this already-shifted position. The result is directional movement rather than isolated fluctuation. The system does not return to prior alignment. It continues forward from each adjusted baseline.

Because this process is incremental, drift does not announce itself through immediate failure. That is what makes it structurally difficult to detect. Financial systems are designed, in part, to absorb variation. Stable systems contain margin, liquidity, and flexibility precisely so that minor disturbances do not interrupt operation. Drift develops inside that absorptive capacity. The same features that allow a system to remain stable in the face of small variation also allow gradual misalignment to proceed without visible signal. Drift therefore uses the system's own tolerance to conceal the early stages of degradation.

This does not mean drift occurs within isolated components. It operates across the entire system. A localized change becomes drift only when it participates in a broader directional shift in system relationships. Income timing alone is not drift. Expense variation alone is not drift. Liquidity decline alone is not drift. Exposure concentration alone is not drift. Drift emerges when distributed changes across these components accumulate into a system-level movement away from alignment. It is the aggregate expression of uncoordinated change.

This system-wide character distinguishes drift from localized disruption. A disruption is bounded. It occurs within a specific component or event channel and can be identified as such. Drift is distributed. No single deviation needs to be large. No individual component needs to fail. The system changes through the interaction of many small shifts that remain tolerable in isolation but become significant in aggregate. Drift is therefore not best understood as a series of problems. It is better understood as a directional process in which the overall configuration becomes less stable over time.

The aggregate nature of drift also explains why it is often misread. Systems are commonly evaluated component by component. Income may still appear adequate. Expenses may still appear manageable. Liquidity may still exist. Exposure may still seem acceptable. Each component can remain within a plausible range while the combined relationship between them deteriorates. Drift is present when the system as a whole has moved into a weaker position even though no single component appears to have crossed a dramatic threshold. The mechanism therefore requires system-level interpretation rather than isolated observation.

Its implication for stability is direct. Drift represents progressive loss of alignment without immediate instability. A system can remain operational while becoming increasingly fragile because stability degradation occurs before failure becomes visible. The absence of visible instability does not mean the absence of structural deterioration. It means that the system still possesses enough remaining tolerance to absorb the consequences of accumulated deviation. But that tolerance is being reduced during the process. Drift narrows margin before it produces breakdown.

This is why operational continuity cannot be treated as proof of preserved stability. A system can continue to function because current variation remains within shrinking margins. Yet the same continuity masks the fact that those margins are no longer what they were. Load may be closer to capacity. Liquidity may be thinner relative to obligation timing. Exposure may be more concentrated relative to the system's tolerance. The system appears stable because it has not failed, but it is not as stable as its continuity suggests. Drift changes the meaning of continued operation. It turns continuity from evidence of alignment into an ambiguous signal that must be interpreted structurally.

The accumulation of deviation over time can be understood as a curve rather than a straight line. In the earliest phase, the curve appears shallow because deviations are small and the system absorbs them with little visible consequence. As additional deviations are incorporated into the operating baseline, the curve bends upward. The system is no longer absorbing variation from its original aligned position, but from a progressively weakened one. The amount of visible stress may still remain limited, yet the structural distance from prior alignment is increasing. Over time, the curve steepens because each additional deviation is being absorbed by a system with less remaining tolerance than before.

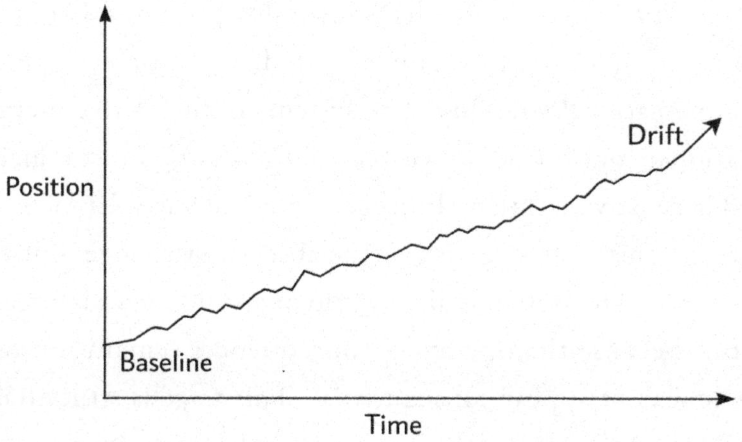

[Figure 1: Drift Accumulation Over Time]

The significance of the curve is not simply that deviation grows. It is that the slope represents changing system sensitivity. A shallow slope indicates that misalignment is accumulating within available tolerance. A steeper slope indicates that the same class of deviations now produces greater structural displacement because the system's margin has been reduced. Increasing slope therefore reflects accelerating misalignment, not necessarily because deviations are larger, but because the system has become less capable of absorbing them. This is the connection between accumulation and instability. Drift reduces tolerance first, and once tolerance is sufficiently compressed, instability emerges from variation that would previously have been absorbed.

The temporal progression of the Drift Mechanism makes this dynamic clearer. In the early stage, drift is largely invisible. Small deviations occur continuously across system components, but they remain below the threshold of observable impact. Income timing may vary modestly, but liquidity still covers timing differences. Expenses may edge upward, but capacity still exceeds load with adequate margin. Liquidity may contract somewhat, but not enough to constrain operations. Exposure may become somewhat more concentrated, but not enough to produce immediate vulnerability. The system continues to function with operational continuity. No visible failure occurs. Drift remains undetected because variation is absorbed inside existing tolerance.

What defines this early stage is not the absence of change, but the absence of signal. The system is already moving. Alignment is already eroding. But because the operating consequences remain limited, the change does not appear consequential. This stage is structurally deceptive. The system seems stable not because alignment is preserved, but because enough margin remains to conceal the effect of its erosion. Drift in this stage is low-visibility directional change.

In the mid stage, the accumulated deviations begin to alter system relationships in ways that compress margin and increase sensitivity. Liquidity is narrower relative to load than it was before. Income variability begins to matter more because less temporal buffer exists to absorb it. Expense variation consumes a larger share of capacity, reducing flexibility. Exposure concentration becomes more significant because the system has less tolerance for localized weakness. The system remains operational, but it does so with reduced room for variation. This is the stage in which drift becomes structurally significant even if it still lacks a clear visible signal.

The defining condition of the mid stage is accumulation that has become consequential without yet becoming catastrophic. The system is closer to its tolerance limits. It does not fail under normal conditions, but it now depends more heavily on normal conditions continuing. Operational continuity remains possible, yet it is achieved from a weaker structural position. Small disturbances that would previously have been neutral now create intermittent pressure. Timing mismatches become more relevant. Buffer depletion matters more. Sensitivity rises. Drift in this stage is no longer merely directional movement; it is directional movement that has materially reduced the system's capacity to remain stable under variation.

In the late stage, accumulated drift reaches the point at which normal variability produces instability. The system no longer absorbs routine deviations with continuity. Instead, those deviations begin to transmit through the structure as sustained stress, constraint, or failure. Income timing variation that once produced no visible effect now creates direct pressure because liquidity is insufficient relative to current load. Expense variability that was once manageable now compresses capacity beyond tolerance. Concentrated exposure amplifies adverse conditions because the system lacks sufficient margin to absorb localized weakness. Instability emerges not because an extraordinary event has occurred, but because prolonged accumulation has altered the configuration of the system so extensively that normal variation has become destabilizing.

This is the final expression of the mechanism. Drift does not require a triggering event because the direction of movement itself is sufficient. A system can move from stability to instability through prolonged accumulation of small deviations that were each absorbed at the time they occurred. Late-stage instability is therefore the visible outcome of a process that began long before any visible interruption. The mechanism explains why instability can appear sudden even when its structural formation has been gradual. What appears sudden at the surface is often the moment at which accumulated drift exceeds remaining tolerance.

The failure condition of the Drift Mechanism is undetected and uncorrected drift. Failure does not begin when the system first becomes unstable. It begins when accumulated deviation is allowed to continue without recognition or adjustment. The visible emergence of instability is simply the point at which the system can no longer absorb the consequences of that accumulation. By that point, the system has already moved substantially away from stable alignment.

This failure condition is defined by the absence of correction, not by the presence of a dramatic event. A system can deteriorate into instability even when no singular disruption explains the transition. That is the structural importance of drift. It converts distributed, low-visibility changes into system-level instability through prolonged accumulation. The system does not need to be struck by a distinct shock to fail. It can instead arrive at instability through its own uncorrected evolution.

The Drift Mechanism therefore explains how financial systems lose alignment in ways that remain hidden during much of the process. It describes a form of degradation that is gradual, directional, and distributed across the entire system. Drift does not interrupt operation at the moment it begins. It allows continuity while reducing the conditions that make continuity stable. That is why it is so consequential. The system continues to function as it becomes less capable of functioning safely.

Drift does not produce immediate failure, which makes detection necessary before instability emerges.

The Lag Mechanism

The Lag Mechanism defines the structural delay between actual changes in system state and the recognition or awareness of those changes. A financial system evolves in real time. Income flows adjust as they are received or interrupted. Expenses change as obligations shift in timing and magnitude. Liquidity rises or falls with each inflow and outflow. Exposure alters as positions accumulate or contract. These changes occur continuously and immediately within the system itself. Awareness of those changes, however, does not occur in real time. It depends on observation, reporting, and interpretation, all of which operate with delay. The result is a persistent gap between the system as it exists and the system as it is perceived.

This gap is structural rather than incidental. It does not arise from occasional oversight or temporary inattention. It arises because the processes through which system state is known are inherently delayed relative to the processes through which system state changes. The system does not wait to be observed before it evolves. It continues to move while observation lags behind. The Lag Mechanism therefore establishes that perception is always a trailing representation of reality. The system state is always ahead of the perceived state.

This distinction creates two parallel conditions within the same system. One is the actual state, defined by the real-time configuration of income, expenses, liquidity, and exposure. The other is the perceived state, defined by the most recent available information and its interpretation. These two states are not identical. The difference between them is the lag. The mechanism is concerned with how that difference forms, how it persists, and how it affects system stability.

The operation of the Lag Mechanism begins with the continuous movement of system components. Income does not arrive as a uniform, perfectly predictable stream. It varies in timing and magnitude, sometimes subtly and sometimes more significantly. Expenses do not remain constant. They fluctuate with timing mismatches, incremental increases, and structural adjustments in obligations. Liquidity is constantly changing as resources are used or replenished. Exposure evolves as positions become more or less concentrated. Each of these changes occurs in real time as part of the system's normal operation.

Awareness of these changes depends on signals. These signals are not instantaneous reflections of system state. They are mediated through reporting cycles, observation intervals, and interpretive processes. Reporting cycles define when information is aggregated and presented. Observation intervals define how frequently the system is reviewed. Interpretive processes determine how observed data is translated into an understanding of system position. Each of these introduces delay. Information is collected after changes have occurred. It is reviewed at discrete points rather than continuously. It is interpreted after it is observed. The perceived state is therefore constructed from data that reflects the system as it existed in the recent past rather than the present moment.

This delay is not uniform across components. Income variability may be recognized only after a sequence of payments has been observed. Expense changes may be identified after patterns emerge over multiple periods. Liquidity shifts may be tracked with varying frequency depending on monitoring practices. Exposure changes may be understood only after aggregation across positions. The result is that different aspects of system state may be perceived with different delays. The perceived state is therefore not only delayed relative to reality, but also uneven in its representation of different components.

Because the system continues to evolve during these delays, the perceived state is always incomplete. It captures a prior configuration rather than the current one. Decisions and adjustments that rely on this perceived state are therefore based on information that lags behind the system's actual position. The Lag Mechanism does not require incorrect interpretation of available data. It operates even when interpretation is accurate relative to the data. The issue is that the data itself reflects a past state. Accuracy of interpretation does not eliminate the delay between reality and awareness.

The relationship between actual system state and perceived state can be understood as two lines evolving over time. The actual system state changes continuously, reflecting real-time adjustments in income, expenses, liquidity, and exposure. The perceived state follows this path with delay, updating only when new information is observed and interpreted. At any given point, the perceived state is positioned behind the actual state. The distance between these two lines represents the lag. As the system evolves, this distance can remain small or expand, depending on the speed of change relative to the speed of detection.

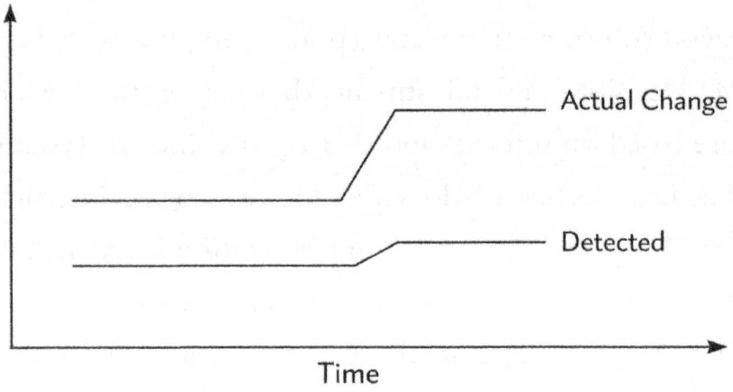

[Figure 2: System Change vs Detection Delay]

The gap between the two lines in the figure represents the magnitude of lag at any point in time. When the gap is narrow, the perceived state closely approximates the actual state. Awareness is relatively aligned with reality, and decisions based on that awareness are more likely to correspond to current conditions. When the gap widens, the perceived state becomes increasingly detached from the actual state. Awareness reflects conditions that no longer exist. The system has already moved beyond the position that is being observed and interpreted. The widening gap therefore represents reduced control. As lag increases, the ability to respond effectively to system changes decreases because responses are based on outdated representations of system position.

The Lag Mechanism operates across the entire system because it affects how all component changes are perceived and interpreted. It does not alter the underlying movement of income, expenses, liquidity, or exposure. Instead, it alters the relationship between that movement and awareness of it. This creates a distortion layer between reality and perception.

Monitoring processes rely on perceived state to evaluate alignment. Decision processes rely on perceived state to determine adjustments. When lag is present, both monitoring and decision-making are based on information that does not fully reflect current conditions.

This distortion influences system interaction by creating a mismatch between actual position and perceived position. The system may have already shifted toward reduced margin, increased sensitivity, or altered exposure, but these changes may not yet be fully recognized. Monitoring may indicate that conditions remain within acceptable bounds because it reflects a prior state in which alignment was stronger. Decisions made under this perception are therefore calibrated to outdated conditions. Adjustments may be insufficient, delayed, or misaligned with the system's current needs.

The Lag Mechanism therefore affects not only awareness but also the timing and effectiveness of response. A system that is monitored with delay will respond with delay. Even if the intention is to maintain alignment, the delay in recognizing deviation allows that deviation to persist and accumulate. By the time a response is initiated, the system may have moved further away from alignment than the perceived state suggests. The response is therefore applied to a condition that no longer exists, reducing its effectiveness.

The implication for stability is that lag introduces structural risk by delaying response to deviation. Stability depends on maintaining alignment between system components as they evolve. When awareness of change is delayed, alignment is not evaluated in real time. Deviation is allowed to accumulate before it is recognized. Even when monitoring is present, the delay between actual change and perceived change creates a window during which the system moves without correction. This window is the period in which misalignment develops.

Lag therefore does not require absence of monitoring to affect stability. It operates within monitored systems as well. The presence of monitoring does not eliminate delay. It only defines the frequency and structure of observation. If the system changes more rapidly than it is observed and interpreted, lag persists. Stability is compromised not only by the existence of deviation but by the delay in recognizing and responding to that deviation. The mechanism establishes that timely awareness is a condition for effective control. Without it, control processes act on outdated information.

The temporal progression of the Lag Mechanism describes how this gap between actual state and perceived state evolves over time.

In the early stage, the awareness gap is minimal relative to system tolerance. Changes in income, expenses, liquidity, and exposure occur, but the delay in recognizing these changes is small compared to the system's capacity to absorb variation. The perceived state remains close to the actual state. Monitoring captures most changes with sufficient proximity to their occurrence that adjustments, if needed, can be made before misalignment becomes significant. The system continues to operate effectively because the lag does not materially distort the understanding of system position. Alignment is maintained because awareness remains sufficiently current relative to system movement.

What defines this stage is not the absence of lag, but its limited impact. The system still evolves ahead of perception, but the difference between the two remains within tolerable bounds. Decisions based on perceived state remain broadly aligned with actual conditions. The system's tolerance absorbs the effect of minor delays in recognition. Lag exists, but it does not yet compromise stability.

In the mid stage, the awareness gap begins to expand. The delay between actual system changes and their recognition increases relative to the system's tolerance. This expansion may result from increased variability in system components, reduced frequency of observation, or greater complexity in interpreting available information. Changes accumulate more rapidly than they are recognized. The perceived state begins to diverge from the actual state in a way that is no longer negligible.

At this stage, monitoring reflects only a partial representation of system position. Some changes are captured, but others remain unobserved or are recognized only after additional delay. The system has already moved beyond the conditions represented in the available information. Decisions made based on this information are therefore calibrated to an outdated configuration. Adjustments may be initiated, but they are applied to a system that has already shifted further. The effectiveness of these adjustments is reduced because they do not fully address the current state of misalignment.

The defining characteristic of the mid stage is partial awareness. The system is no longer being interpreted with sufficient accuracy to maintain alignment, but the gap has not yet become fully destabilizing. Misalignment is allowed to persist because it is not fully recognized. Lag in this stage contributes to the accumulation of deviation by delaying the initiation of corrective processes.

In the late stage, the awareness gap becomes structurally significant. The system has evolved to a point where its actual configuration differs materially from its perceived configuration. The perceived state no longer provides a reliable basis for evaluating alignment or determining appropriate adjustments. By the time changes are recognized, the system has already moved into a weakened or unstable position.

At this stage, responses occur after misalignment has become consequential. The system may already be operating with compressed margins, increased sensitivity, or constrained liquidity when these conditions are identified. Adjustments initiated at this point are reactive rather than preventive. They are constrained by the system's reduced flexibility and may be insufficient to restore alignment fully. The delay between change and recognition has allowed misalignment to develop beyond the point where it can be easily corrected.

The late stage therefore represents a condition in which lag has compromised control. The system continues to evolve, but awareness is no longer sufficiently aligned with that evolution to support effective intervention. Instability emerges not only because deviation exists, but because the delay in recognizing that deviation has allowed it to accumulate unchecked.

The boundary condition of the Lag Mechanism is delayed recognition of accumulated change. Failure occurs when the system state has already degraded beyond stable conditions before this degradation is detected. At that point, responses are necessarily reactive. They address consequences rather than preventing their formation. The system's ability to maintain stability is reduced because the timing of intervention is misaligned with the timing of change.

This failure condition is defined by the gap between reality and awareness. When that gap becomes large enough, the system effectively operates without accurate feedback. Monitoring no longer reflects current conditions. Decisions no longer correspond to actual needs. Control processes lose their ability to maintain alignment because they are based on information that does not represent the present state of the system.

The Lag Mechanism therefore establishes that awareness is not simultaneous with change. It is delayed, and that delay has structural consequences. The system evolves continuously, but perception updates intermittently. The difference between these two processes creates a gap that influences monitoring, decision-making, and adjustment. As that gap widens, the ability to maintain stability diminishes.

Lag obscures the true state of the system, making accurate detection necessary for maintaining alignment.

The Invisible Degradation Mechanism

The Invisible Degradation Mechanism defines the condition in which a financial system continues to function operationally while its underlying alignment deteriorates. Functioning and stability are not equivalent states. A system can maintain uninterrupted operation—income is received, expenses are paid, liquidity is present, and obligations are met—while the relationships that support stable operation weaken beneath that continuity. The mechanism establishes that observable functionality does not confirm structural integrity. It only confirms that the system has not yet reached the point where misalignment produces visible disruption.

At any moment, a financial system can be evaluated along two distinct dimensions. The first is operational function, which reflects whether the system continues to perform its immediate processes. The second is structural alignment, which reflects whether the relationships between system components remain within the bounds required for stability. These dimensions do not move in parallel. A system can remain fully functional while its structural alignment deteriorates. The Invisible Degradation Mechanism exists within the divergence between these two conditions.

Operational function is visible. It is expressed through continuity of inflows, completion of outflows, and the absence of interruption. Structural alignment is not directly visible. It is defined by relationships—between income and expenses, liquidity and obligations, exposure and tolerance—that determine how the system behaves under variation. These relationships can change without interrupting function. As long as the system retains enough capacity to meet its immediate demands, function persists. Alignment, however, may already be shifting in a direction that reduces the system's ability to sustain that function over time.

The mechanism operates through the capacity of systems to preserve short-term functionality while absorbing changes that degrade long-term alignment. Income may continue to arrive, even if its variability increases. Expenses may continue to be paid, even if their baseline rises relative to capacity. Liquidity may remain present, even if it becomes less proportional to the system's obligations. Exposure may remain within tolerable conditions, even as it becomes more concentrated. Each of these shifts can occur without interrupting operation. The system continues to function, and that continuity masks the underlying change.

This masking effect is central to the mechanism. Operational success becomes a signal that is interpreted as stability, even when structural conditions are weakening. Because function is observable and alignment is not, evaluation defaults to what can be seen. If the system continues to operate without disruption, it is assumed to be stable. The mechanism establishes that this assumption is structurally unreliable. Function is a lagging indicator of alignment. It persists after alignment has begun to deteriorate because the system still contains sufficient margin to absorb the effects of that deterioration.

The preservation of function under weakening alignment depends on margin. Margin represents the system's capacity to absorb variation without failure. As long as margin exists, the system can continue to operate even as its underlying relationships degrade. However, margin is not static. It is reduced as alignment deteriorates. The system continues to function, but it does so from a progressively weaker position. The same operational outcomes are achieved, but with less tolerance for variation.

This creates a condition in which function becomes decoupled from structural health. The system appears stable because it continues to meet its obligations, but the conditions that support that stability are eroding. This decoupling is not temporary or anomalous. It is an inherent property of systems that possess absorptive capacity. The ability to absorb variation allows the system to maintain function in the presence of degradation. It also delays the visibility of that degradation.

The Invisible Degradation Mechanism operates at the level of relationships rather than individual components. It does not require failure within income, expenses, liquidity, or exposure. Each component can remain within acceptable ranges while their relationships shift in ways that reduce alignment. Income may still exceed expenses, but the margin between them may narrow. Liquidity may still exist, but it may no longer be sufficient relative to the timing and magnitude of obligations. Exposure may still appear manageable, but it may be more concentrated than before. These changes do not interrupt function, but they alter the system's structural position.

This distinction clarifies the difference between a functioning system and an aligned system. A functioning system is defined by continuity of operation. It performs its processes without interruption. An aligned system is defined by the stability of its relationships. It maintains sufficient margin, appropriate distribution of load, adequate liquidity relative to obligation, and controlled exposure relative to tolerance. A system can satisfy the conditions of function without satisfying the conditions of alignment. The mechanism exists within this divergence.

Because function is maintained, degradation remains hidden. There is no immediate signal that indicates a loss of alignment. The system does not produce visible feedback when relationships weaken, as long as operational demands continue to be met. This absence of signal allows degradation to proceed without recognition. The system adapts to its changing configuration, incorporating weaker relationships into its operating baseline without identifying them as problematic.

The implication for stability is that surface indicators cannot be relied upon to assess structural condition. Continued income, timely expense payment, and the presence of liquidity do not confirm alignment. They confirm only that the system has not yet reached a point where misalignment disrupts function. Stability must therefore be evaluated based on the relationships that define alignment rather than the continuity that defines function. The mechanism establishes that surface stability can conceal structural instability.

This concealment is reinforced by the way systems are typically observed. Evaluation tends to focus on discrete outcomes rather than underlying relationships. If obligations are met and resources remain available, the system is considered stable. The Invisible Degradation Mechanism demonstrates that this mode of evaluation is incomplete. It does not capture the gradual erosion of alignment that occurs beneath continued operation. By the time structural instability becomes visible through functional disruption, the degradation that caused it has already progressed significantly.

The temporal progression of the mechanism describes how this hidden degradation develops over time.

In the early stage, the system exhibits full surface stability. All observable functions continue without interruption. Income is received according to expectation, expenses are paid without strain, liquidity appears sufficient to support operations, and exposure remains within acceptable limits. Degradation begins through small shifts in the relationships between these components. Expenses may increase slightly relative to income. Liquidity may decline modestly relative to obligations. Exposure may become marginally more concentrated. These changes do not produce visible signals because they remain within the system's existing margin. Stability is inferred from uninterrupted operation, and no distinction is made between function and alignment. Degradation is present but not observable.

What defines this stage is the absence of contradiction between perception and operation. The system appears stable because it functions, and there is no visible evidence to challenge that interpretation. Alignment is already beginning to erode, but the system's absorptive capacity conceals the effect of that erosion. Function and perceived stability remain aligned, even though structural alignment has begun to diverge.

In the mid stage, hidden misalignment becomes more pronounced. The relationships between system components weaken in ways that reduce margin and increase sensitivity. Income may still cover expenses, but with less excess capacity. Liquidity may still exist, but it may no longer provide the same temporal coverage relative to obligations. Exposure may become more concentrated, increasing the system's reliance on specific conditions remaining favorable. The system continues to function, but this functionality depends increasingly on those favorable conditions.

The defining characteristic of this stage is that degradation has become structurally significant while remaining operationally concealed. The system's ability to absorb variation is reduced, but variation has not yet exceeded the reduced tolerance. As a result, no visible failure occurs. The system appears stable, but its stability is conditional. It depends on the absence of disruption. The underlying relationships no longer support the same level of resilience, but this change is not reflected in surface indicators. Function persists, and because function persists, stability is assumed.

In the late stage, structural instability develops beneath continued functionality. The system reaches a point where its underlying relationships are no longer aligned with the conditions required for stable operation. Margin has been sufficiently reduced that normal variability approaches or exceeds the system's tolerance. Liquidity may be present but insufficient relative to the timing and magnitude of obligations. Income may continue but with variability that the system can no longer absorb.

Exposure may be concentrated to a degree that amplifies the effect of adverse conditions. The system continues to function, but it does so from a structurally unstable position.

At this stage, functionality is fragile. It persists, but it is highly sensitive to variation. The system appears stable at the surface, but it is no longer capable of maintaining that stability under normal conditions. Instability is imminent, but it has not yet fully manifested. The absence of visible failure creates the impression that stability remains intact, even though the system's structural capacity to sustain that stability has been compromised.

The transition from this stage to visible instability occurs when normal variability exceeds the reduced tolerance created by accumulated degradation. The system does not gradually signal this transition through incremental failure. Instead, it may appear to move abruptly from stable operation to disruption. This apparent abruptness is the result of hidden degradation reaching a point where it can no longer be absorbed. The system's surface continuity conceals the buildup of structural weakness until that weakness becomes impossible to contain.

The boundary condition of the Invisible Degradation Mechanism is reliance on surface indicators of stability while underlying alignment has deteriorated. Failure occurs when evaluation is based solely on observable function, allowing hidden degradation to proceed without recognition or correction. By the time instability becomes visible, the system has already undergone substantial structural weakening. The emergence of failure is therefore not the beginning of instability, but its revelation.

This failure condition reflects the separation between function and alignment. A system that is evaluated only through its ability to continue operating will not detect degradation until it produces visible disruption. At that point, the system's margin has already been reduced, its sensitivity increased, and its flexibility constrained. The ability to restore alignment is limited because the system is no longer operating from a position of strength.

The Invisible Degradation Mechanism establishes that stability cannot be inferred from continuity. It must be evaluated through the relationships that define alignment. Systems can maintain surface stability while becoming structurally unstable, and this divergence can persist for extended periods without visible signal. The absence of failure does not confirm the presence of stability. It confirms only that the system has not yet reached the point where hidden degradation produces observable consequence.

Visibility must therefore be constructed rather than assumed, because system degradation can occur without observable failure.

The Control Loop Mechanism

The Control Loop Mechanism defines the continuous process through which a financial system is observed, evaluated, and adjusted in response to its current state. Stability is not maintained through isolated decisions or occasional interventions. It is maintained through repetition. The mechanism establishes that control is not a singular act applied to the system. It is an ongoing cycle that operates as long as the system itself operates. Without this cycle, the system reverts to passive behavior, allowing the processes described in earlier chapters—decay, drift, lag, and invisible degradation—to proceed without interruption.

A financial system exists in motion. Income changes, expenses adjust, liquidity fluctuates, and exposure shifts continuously. These changes alter the system's configuration in real time. The Control Loop Mechanism exists to maintain alignment within that movement. It does so by converting system activity into feedback and then converting that feedback into adjustment. This conversion is not discrete. It does not occur at a single point in time. It is cyclical, repeating continuously as the system evolves.

The mechanism is defined by a sequence: observe, evaluate, adjust, and repeat. Observation captures the current state of the system. Evaluation interprets that state relative to the conditions required for alignment. Adjustment modifies the system to restore or preserve alignment. The final element—repeat—returns the process to observation, creating a continuous loop rather than a linear sequence. The system is not observed once. It is observed continuously. It is not adjusted once. It is adjusted as often as required to maintain alignment. The loop does not end because the system does not stop changing.

Observation is the entry point of the loop. It represents the process through which system state becomes visible. Income flows are tracked in terms of timing and magnitude. Expenses are observed in terms of baseline, variability, and obligation structure. Liquidity is monitored in relation to current and projected demands. Exposure is assessed in terms of distribution and concentration. Observation does not alter the system. It renders the system's current configuration visible. Without observation, the system operates without feedback. Changes occur, but they are not captured. The system evolves without awareness.

Evaluation follows observation. It interprets observed data relative to alignment conditions. The system is not evaluated based on isolated component performance, but on the relationships between components. Income is assessed relative to expenses. Liquidity is assessed relative to obligations. Exposure is assessed relative to tolerance. Evaluation determines whether these relationships remain within the bounds required for stability. It translates observation into a position: aligned, approaching misalignment, or misaligned. Without evaluation, observation remains descriptive. The system is seen, but not understood in terms of its stability.

Adjustment follows evaluation. It modifies the system's configuration to restore or maintain alignment. Adjustments may involve altering the relationship between capacity and load, redistributing exposure, or recalibrating liquidity relative to obligation. The mechanism does not define the specific form of adjustment. It defines the necessity of adjustment as a response to evaluated state. Adjustment is not reactive to failure. It is applied before instability emerges, based on the detection of deviation from alignment. Without adjustment, evaluation does not influence system behavior. The system continues to evolve without correction.

The final component of the sequence is repetition. The loop returns to observation, and the cycle continues. This repetition is essential because the system does not reach a final state of alignment. It moves continuously. Each adjustment alters the system, and that altered system must be observed again. The Control Loop Mechanism therefore operates without termination. It is sustained as long as the system exists. Stability is maintained through the continuity of the loop, not through the completeness of any single cycle.

The sequence of observe, evaluate, adjust, and repeat forms a closed cycle.

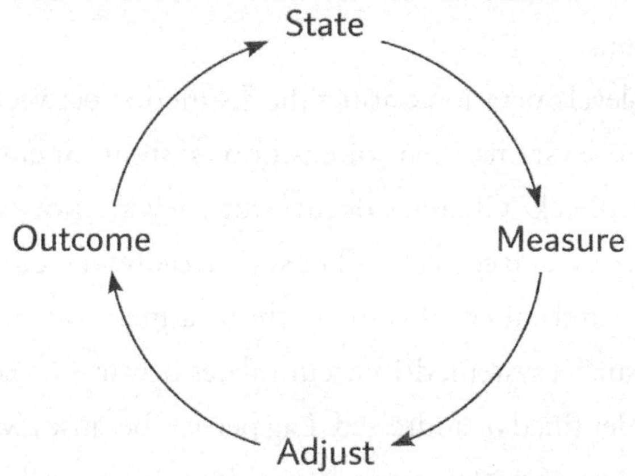

[Figure 3: Financial Control Loop]

The figure represents this cycle as a continuous loop rather than a linear progression. Observation feeds into evaluation, evaluation into adjustment, and adjustment returns the system to observation. The absence of an endpoint reflects the continuous nature of system change.

The loop does not resolve into a stable equilibrium that requires no further action. Instead, it maintains alignment by continuously integrating feedback into system configuration. The repetition of the loop is not redundant. It is the mechanism through which alignment is preserved over time. Each iteration updates the system's configuration in response to its current state, preventing the accumulation of uncorrected deviation.

The Control Loop Mechanism operates across the entire system by integrating feedback from all components into a unified process of control. Income variability, expense shifts, liquidity movement, and exposure changes are not managed independently. They are observed and evaluated in relation to one another. This integration distinguishes the control loop from isolated decision-making. Decisions may adjust individual components, but the control loop adjusts the relationships between components. It operates at the system level rather than at the level of individual actions.

This system-level operation clarifies the distinction between closed-loop and open-loop systems. An open-loop system operates without continuous feedback. Changes occur, but they are not systematically observed, evaluated, and corrected. The system evolves based on its internal dynamics and external conditions without a mechanism to maintain alignment. In such a system, drift accumulates because deviations are not continuously identified or addressed. Lag persists because awareness is not updated in alignment with system change. Invisible degradation develops because function is not evaluated relative to structural relationships.

A closed-loop system, by contrast, integrates feedback continuously. Observation captures system state, evaluation interprets that state, and adjustment modifies the system in response. The loop repeats, ensuring that deviations are identified and corrected as they occur. The presence of the loop does not eliminate change. It regulates change by maintaining alignment within evolving conditions. The Control Loop Mechanism is therefore the structure that converts monitoring into control. Without it, monitoring remains passive. With it, monitoring becomes active intervention.

The interaction between the control loop and previously defined mechanisms is direct. Drift represents the accumulation of uncorrected deviation. The control loop interrupts this accumulation by identifying and correcting deviations as they emerge. Lag represents the delay between system change and awareness. The control loop reduces this delay by increasing the frequency and continuity of observation and evaluation. Invisible degradation represents the divergence between functioning and alignment. The control loop resolves this divergence by evaluating structural relationships rather than relying on surface indicators of function. The mechanism does not eliminate these processes. It counteracts them through continuous feedback and adjustment.

The implication for stability is that it depends on the presence of a functioning control loop. Stability is not a property of system configuration alone. It is a property of how that configuration is maintained over time. Without a control loop, the system operates passively. It absorbs changes without evaluating their impact on alignment. Over time, this leads to decay and drift. With a control loop, the system actively maintains alignment. Deviations are identified and corrected before they accumulate into structural misalignment.

This establishes that governance is not an event. It is not a periodic intervention applied when instability becomes visible. It is a continuous process sustained through repeated cycles of feedback and correction. The Control Loop Mechanism defines governance as this process. It is not defined by the content of individual decisions, but by the structure through which decisions are informed and applied. Governance exists where the loop exists. It is absent where the loop is absent.

The effectiveness of the control loop depends on the continuity and integration of its components. Observation must be sufficiently frequent to capture system change. Evaluation must accurately interpret observed data relative to alignment conditions. Adjustment must be applied in response to evaluation, not delayed until instability emerges. Repetition must occur without interruption. Breakdowns in any part of the loop reduce its effectiveness. Irregular observation introduces lag. Incomplete evaluation reduces the accuracy of response. Delayed adjustment allows deviation to accumulate. Disrupted repetition converts the loop into a series of isolated actions.

The temporal progression of the Control Loop Mechanism describes how the loop develops and operates with varying degrees of effectiveness.

In the early stage, the loop exists in an irregular or partial form. Observation may occur, but not consistently. Evaluation may be incomplete, focusing on isolated components rather than system relationships. Adjustments may be made, but they are reactive and not systematically tied to observed state. The sequence of observe, evaluate, and adjust is present, but it is fragmented. The loop does not operate continuously. As a result, feedback is not fully integrated into system behavior. The system retains elements of control, but it also retains characteristics of open-loop operation. Drift and lag are only partially counteracted because the loop is not consistently applied.

The defining characteristic of this stage is inconsistency. The system is observed intermittently, evaluated partially, and adjusted irregularly. Control exists, but it is not continuous. The system's alignment depends on occasional intervention rather than sustained process. This allows periods of passive operation during which deviation can accumulate.

In the mid stage, the control loop becomes structured but operates with delay or inconsistency. Observation occurs regularly, providing a more consistent view of system state. Evaluation is more systematic, interpreting relationships between components rather than isolated data points. Adjustments are made in response to evaluation, but they may not be applied immediately or fully. The loop functions, but with friction.

Delays between observation, evaluation, and adjustment reduce the loop's responsiveness.

At this stage, the system benefits from the presence of a control structure, but the effectiveness of that structure is limited by timing and integration. Feedback is incorporated, but not in real time. Deviations are identified, but correction may lag behind their development. The loop reduces the accumulation of misalignment, but it does not eliminate it entirely. The system operates with partial control, maintaining alignment under stable conditions but becoming more vulnerable as variability increases.

The defining characteristic of the mid stage is delayed integration. The loop exists and functions, but the timing between its components introduces inefficiency. The system is controlled, but not optimally aligned with its real-time state.

In the late stage, the control loop operates continuously with minimal delay between observation, evaluation, and adjustment. Observation captures system state in close alignment with real-time conditions. Evaluation accurately interprets that state relative to alignment requirements. Adjustments are applied promptly, recalibrating the system before deviation accumulates. The loop repeats without interruption, maintaining continuous integration of feedback into system behavior.

At this stage, the system operates as a closed-loop system in full form. Feedback is not merely collected; it is continuously integrated into system configuration. The system maintains alignment not by resisting change, but by adapting to it as it occurs. Deviations are identified early and corrected before they become structurally significant. The loop functions as a stable mechanism for preserving system integrity over time.

The defining characteristic of the late stage is continuity. The loop operates without fragmentation or delay. Control is not episodic. It is sustained. The system remains aligned because it is continuously recalibrated in response to its current state.

The boundary condition of the Control Loop Mechanism is the absence or breakdown of the loop. When the loop does not exist, or when its components fail to operate in sequence, the system reverts to open-loop behavior. Changes occur without continuous observation. Observations occur without evaluation. Evaluations occur without adjustment. Adjustments occur without repetition. In each case, feedback is not fully integrated into system behavior.

In the absence of a functioning loop, the system loses its ability to maintain alignment. Drift accumulates because deviations are not continuously corrected. Lag persists because awareness is not updated in alignment with change. Invisible degradation develops because structural relationships are not evaluated. The system may continue to function, but it does so without active control. Stability degrades over time as misalignment accumulates.

The failure condition is therefore not a single event, but the absence of continuous process. Without the loop, the system cannot maintain alignment because it cannot integrate feedback into its operation. Stability becomes dependent on initial configuration and favorable conditions rather than on sustained control.

The Control Loop Mechanism establishes that maintaining alignment requires structure. Stability is not preserved through isolated actions or periodic review. It is preserved through a continuous and repeatable process that observes system state, evaluates alignment, and adjusts configuration in response. This process must operate without interruption because the system itself does not stop evolving.

Control requires structure, because maintaining alignment depends on a continuous and repeatable process rather than isolated actions.

The Measurement & Signal Mechanism

The Measurement & Signal Mechanism defines the process through which system data is captured and translated into signals that represent system state. Measurement does not directly reveal stability. It does not, by itself, disclose whether a financial system is aligned or misaligned. It produces data. That data must then be organized and interpreted before it can indicate anything about alignment. The mechanism therefore begins with a distinction between system activity and system understanding. Activity occurs continuously through income movement, expense load, liquidity change, and exposure adjustment. Understanding begins only when that activity is measured in a way that can be converted into information.

This makes measurement the input layer of governance. A control loop cannot observe a system in any meaningful way unless system activity is rendered into measurable form. Income must be captured as flow, timing, and variability. Expenses must be measured as load, recurrence, and change in baseline. Liquidity must be measured as accessible balance, depletion rate, and relationship to obligation timing. Exposure must be measured as concentration, distribution, and sensitivity. These measurements do not yet explain the system. They provide the raw material from which explanation becomes possible. The mechanism establishes that control begins not with response, but with structured capture of system activity.

The operation of the mechanism begins with the distinction between raw data and signals. Raw data consists of values, balances, flows, and observed changes. It records what is happening within the system. A balance decreases. An expense rises. Income arrives later than expected. A larger share of system stability becomes dependent on a narrower source of inflow or asset access. These are measurable facts. But facts in isolation do not yet indicate whether the system is moving toward or away from alignment. Signal emerges only when raw data is interpreted as a meaningful pattern, relationship, or deviation. Data records activity. Signal identifies whether that activity matters for stability.

This distinction is necessary because financial systems produce continuous variation. Income does not recur in perfectly identical form across time. Expenses do not remain unchanged from period to period. Liquidity fluctuates through normal use and replenishment. Exposure is rarely fixed in exact proportion. If every variation were treated as equally meaningful, the system would be impossible to monitor coherently. Measurement would produce quantity without structure. The mechanism therefore requires a second distinction: not all measured variation carries the same informational weight. Some variation reflects meaningful changes in alignment. Some variation does not.

Measurement converts system activity into observable data across the full set of operating components. Income measurement captures not only amount, but pattern. A stable nominal inflow with increasing timing irregularity is different from a stable nominal inflow received predictably. Expense measurement captures not only total outflow, but structure. A stable total expense level with greater rigidity or less smoothing capacity represents a different condition than the same total spread across more flexible timing. Liquidity measurement captures not only available balance, but accessibility relative to obligations and consumption rate relative to replenishment. Exposure measurement captures not only what the system is linked to, but how concentrated that linkage has become relative to the system's tolerance. In each case, the function of measurement is to transform movement into visible form.

This is why the mechanism sits directly inside the control loop. Observation depends on measurement. Without measurement, observation remains imprecise. A system may be reviewed, but it cannot be observed structurally unless its activity is captured in organized form. Measurement feeds observation with structured inputs. It provides the informational surface through which the system becomes legible to itself. Without that surface, the control loop lacks definition. It may still react to visible problems, but it cannot monitor alignment continuously because it lacks the underlying data from which signals can be formed.

At the same time, measurement alone is insufficient. Data that is captured but not transformed into signals remains unstructured. It records events without indicating their significance. A system may accumulate balances, statements, flow records, and category totals without producing any meaningful awareness of alignment. The mechanism therefore defines measurement as necessary but incomplete. It is the interface between system activity and system awareness, but awareness requires the further step of signal formation. Data enters the control loop only when it becomes capable of indicating whether system relationships are changing in a meaningful way.

The core distinction between signal and noise emerges at this point. Signal is meaningful variation that reflects changes in system alignment. Noise is variation that does not materially affect system stability. Both appear inside measurement. Both are visible in data. But they are not equivalent. A small fluctuation in expense timing that remains well inside existing liquidity tolerance may be measurable without being significant. A gradual compression between liquidity and obligation timing may appear modest in any single period but represent a meaningful change in system position. Signal and noise therefore cannot be separated by visibility alone. They are separated by whether the variation alters the system's alignment relative to stable operating bounds.

Signal and noise can be understood as variation bands around a baseline. Around any stable operating condition, some degree of movement is normal and non-consequential. Income may vary modestly without changing capacity in a structurally important way. Expenses may move within a limited range without altering load beyond tolerance. Liquidity may fluctuate inside a normal operating band without reducing financial time below functional requirements. Exposure may shift slightly without changing concentration materially. These variations remain inside the noise range. Signal emerges when variation moves outside that range and begins to indicate a meaningful change in alignment rather than ordinary operating movement.

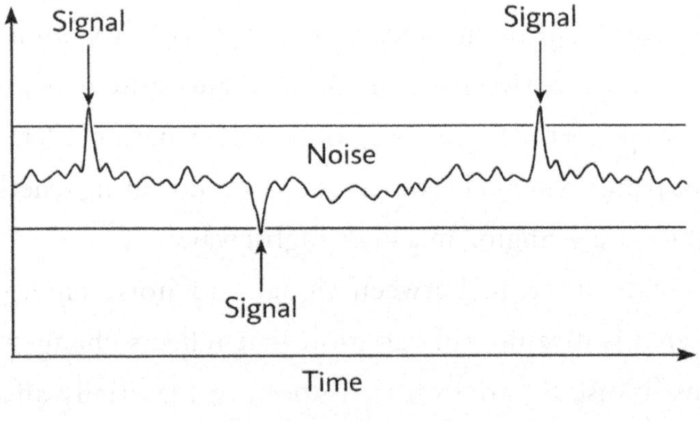

[Figure 4: Signal vs Noise Bands]

The figure represents these bands as thresholds around baseline conditions. Variation inside the inner range is noise because it does not materially change system stability. Variation crossing beyond that range becomes signal because it indicates deviation large enough, persistent enough, or structurally relevant enough to affect alignment.

The importance of the threshold is not that it removes judgment, but that it structures judgment. Signals are not merely larger numbers. They are changes that exceed the system's normal operating band and therefore require interpretive attention inside the control loop. Without thresholds, all variation competes equally for response. With thresholds, meaningful deviation can be distinguished from routine movement.

Measurement becomes ineffective when distortion alters what the data appears to represent. The mechanism therefore includes not only capture and signal formation, but the risk of misrepresentation. Distortion occurs when measurement does not accurately reflect current system state. This can happen through incomplete data, delayed reporting, aggregation effects, or improper framing. Incomplete data omits relevant portions of system activity, producing a partial view that may appear coherent while failing to reflect the whole. Delayed reporting introduces a gap between actual state and measured state, so that the system is interpreted through outdated conditions. Aggregation effects compress multiple distinct movements into a single summary value, concealing changes in structure or timing beneath stable totals. Improper framing organizes data in ways that obscure the relationships that matter for alignment.

Each form of distortion changes the quality of the signals produced. If income is measured only by nominal total, timing instability may remain hidden. If expenses are measured only as aggregate monthly outflow, shifts in rigidity or sequencing may disappear inside an unchanged total. If liquidity is measured only as static balance, its relationship to near-term obligations may be missed. If exposure is measured without concentration, the system may appear diversified in count while remaining concentrated in consequence. Distortion does not require false data. It requires data that is structurally insufficient for representing the condition being evaluated.

This matters because the control loop evaluates based on what measurement presents. If measurement is distorted, observation is degraded at the point of entry. The system may appear stable not because it is stable, but because the data structure fails to reveal meaningful deviation. In that condition, signals are weakened, delayed, or displaced. Noise may appear prominent because the data emphasizes visible fluctuation over structural relevance. Signals may disappear because the data is aggregated or framed in ways that conceal relationship change. The problem is not absence of information. It is failure of information quality.

The distinction between data and meaning follows from this. Data reflects system activity. Meaning reflects system position relative to alignment. Data can show that income declined, expenses increased, liquidity narrowed, or exposure concentrated. Meaning determines whether those changes matter in a way that alters stability. The movement from data to meaning is not automatic. It requires interpretation. The mechanism therefore establishes a sequence: measurement captures activity, signal organizes meaningful variation, and interpretation converts that signal into understanding of system position. Without this final step, measured information remains descriptive but not operational.

This distinction prevents two common failures. The first is accumulation without understanding. A system may gather more and more data while remaining unable to determine whether alignment is improving or degrading. The second is reaction without meaning. A system may respond to visible changes without knowing whether those changes are signal or noise. In both cases, measurement exists, but monitoring remains weak because data has not been converted into meaningful system awareness. The mechanism does not define interpretation itself in full depth, but it establishes why interpretation is necessary. Measurement alone does not define alignment. It only supplies the material from which alignment can be inferred.

The stability implication is therefore clear. Stability depends not on raw data accumulation, but on accurate signal detection. A system can measure extensively and still fail if it cannot distinguish noise from meaningful deviation. Likewise, a system can detect meaningful variation but fail if distortion weakens or delays the signal. Effective monitoring requires structured measurement that captures the right system variables and organizes them in a way that allows meaningful deviation to be recognized. Stability is not protected by data volume. It is protected by measurement quality and signal accuracy.

When noise is mistaken for signal, control becomes unstable in a different way. The system begins to react to ordinary variation as though it reflected structural change. Adjustment becomes misdirected because it is triggered by movement that does not materially affect alignment. When signal is mistaken for noise, the opposite failure occurs. Meaningful deviation is absorbed into normal variation and therefore goes unaddressed. In both cases, the control loop is weakened at the point of input. Observation becomes unreliable because the informational boundary between routine movement and relevant change is not properly drawn.

The temporal progression of the mechanism clarifies how measurement quality develops. In the early stage, measurement is unstructured. Data is collected inconsistently or without clear signal definition. Income, expenses, liquidity, and exposure may all be visible in fragments, but the system lacks a coherent way to distinguish meaningful variation from routine movement. Monitoring exists in a loose sense, but it lacks precision. The system can see activity, yet it cannot reliably identify which changes matter for alignment. Signal and noise remain intermixed.

In the mid stage, measurement becomes more structured, but signal identification remains imperfect. Data is collected more consistently and organized more clearly across system components. Thresholds or comparative baselines begin to form. However, distortion still affects interpretation. Noise may be treated as signal because visible fluctuation receives disproportionate weight. Signals may be overlooked because delays, aggregation, or framing still weaken their visibility. Monitoring improves, but the system remains vulnerable to misclassification. The input layer of control exists, but it does not yet produce stable informational quality.

In the late stage, measurement is structured and aligned with the underlying system. Income, expenses, liquidity, and exposure are captured in forms that reflect their actual role in stability. Raw data is organized into signals that distinguish meaningful deviation from routine variation. Noise remains visible, but it is not confused with alignment change. Distortion is reduced because data is timely enough, complete enough, and framed around the relationships that matter. At this stage, monitoring becomes effective because measurement supports accurate evaluation rather than merely recording activity.

The boundary condition of the mechanism is failure to generate meaningful signals. This can occur through absence of adequate measurement or through inability to distinguish signal from noise. In either case, the control loop receives degraded input. Observation becomes imprecise, evaluation becomes unreliable, and adjustment becomes delayed or incorrect. Instability then emerges not because data was unavailable in a general sense, but because the system lacked a valid informational representation of its own condition.

The Measurement & Signal Mechanism therefore establishes the first requirement of effective monitoring. System activity must be captured in structured form, meaningful variation must be distinguished from routine movement, and the resulting signals must accurately represent changes in alignment. Measurement alone is insufficient because data is not yet signal, and signal alone is insufficient because signal is not yet meaning. But without measurement, neither signal nor meaning can emerge at all.

Signals require interpretation because measurement alone does not define system alignment.

The Threshold & Trigger Mechanism

The Threshold & Trigger Mechanism defines the process through which measured signals are evaluated against defined limits to determine when variation requires action. A financial system does not maintain stability by responding to every observed change. Continuous variation is normal within any operating system. Income timing shifts, expenses fluctuate, liquidity levels move, and exposure changes in degree rather than remaining fixed. If every movement generated response, the system would become unstable through overcorrection. If no movement generated response, misalignment would accumulate without interruption. The mechanism therefore establishes a conditional structure between observation and adjustment. Variation becomes actionable only when it exceeds defined limits.

This is the point at which signal is converted into response. Measurement produces data. Signal identifies meaningful deviation. Thresholds determine whether that deviation remains within acceptable bounds or has moved beyond them. Triggers determine when crossing those bounds initiates action. The mechanism is therefore not about detection alone. It is about structured response. It defines how a system distinguishes between conditions that can be absorbed and conditions that require recalibration.

The operation of the mechanism begins with the recognition that stability is not a fixed point. A financial system is not aligned only when every variable rests at a precise value. Stability exists across a range of conditions within which the relationships between income, expenses, liquidity, and exposure remain functionally aligned. Income may vary modestly while still supporting obligations. Expenses may fluctuate within a bounded range without overwhelming capacity. Liquidity may move up and down without compromising temporal coverage. Exposure may shift within acceptable limits without exceeding tolerance. Alignment therefore exists within a zone, not at a single coordinate.

Thresholds define the boundaries of that zone. They mark the point at which variation stops being absorbable within existing structure and begins to indicate meaningful deviation from stable operating conditions. A threshold is not failure. It is the limit beyond which the system is no longer operating within its defined range of acceptable variation. Before that limit, the system absorbs movement. Beyond that limit, the system requires adjustment to preserve alignment. The threshold therefore separates tolerated movement from actionable deviation.

Triggers operate after thresholds are defined. A threshold identifies the boundary. A trigger defines the condition under which a threshold breach becomes an instruction for action. This distinction is necessary because the existence of a boundary does not by itself produce response. The system must also determine how threshold crossing is translated into intervention. A trigger is that translation. It converts evaluated deviation into a control response. Without triggers, thresholds remain conceptual. Without thresholds, triggers become arbitrary. The mechanism depends on both.

Its operation can be understood as a sequence. Signals are generated through measurement and interpretation. Those signals are then compared against stability ranges and tolerance bands. If the signal remains within tolerance, no action is required because the variation is being absorbed within stable limits. If the signal crosses the defined threshold, a trigger condition is met, and adjustment becomes necessary. Response is therefore conditional rather than continuous. The system does not react to all movement. It reacts to movement that has been structured as meaningful relative to defined limits.

This mechanism sits at the decision interface within the control loop. Measurement provides input. Evaluation interprets system position. The Threshold & Trigger Mechanism determines whether that position requires adjustment. Without thresholds, the control loop cannot regulate response coherently. It will either overreact or underreact. Overreaction occurs when routine variation is treated as though it were destabilizing. Underreaction occurs when meaningful deviation is treated as though it were still within acceptable range. The mechanism prevents both errors by structuring the conversion from signal to action.

The distinction between stability range and tolerance band is central to this structure. The stability range is the operating zone within which the relationships that define system alignment remain intact. It is the area in which the system is functioning with sufficient margin, proportionality, and tolerable exposure. The tolerance band is the acceptable variation around that range that does not require action. It recognizes that even within a stable system, movement occurs. Stability is therefore not a single narrow state but a bounded operating band in which deviation can be absorbed without recalibration.

A stable financial system must therefore be understood as occupying a band rather than a point. It does not move from stable to unstable at the first sign of change. It remains stable through limited variation because its structure can absorb that variation without loss of alignment. The threshold sits at the outer boundary of this band. Inside the inner operating range, the system remains aligned. Within the surrounding tolerance band, the system still remains absorbent and does not require response. Once movement exceeds that outer boundary, the system has crossed from absorbable variation into meaningful deviation.

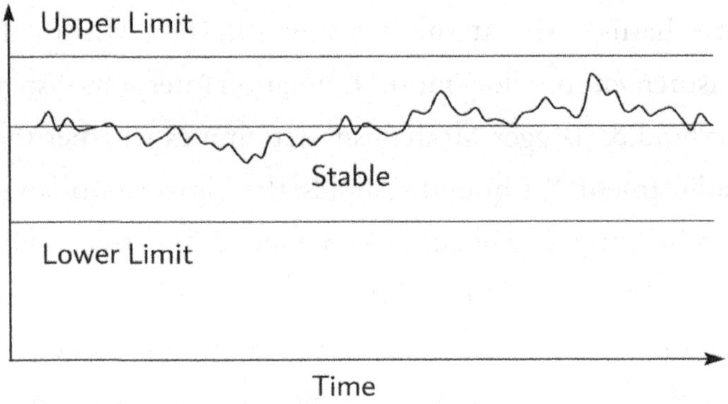

[Figure 5: Stability Threshold Bands]

The figure represents stability as layered bands rather than a single target line. The inner band is the stable operating range in which alignment is preserved under ordinary conditions. The outer boundary marks the threshold beyond which variation is no longer being safely absorbed. Movement beyond that boundary is not yet failure, but it is a trigger condition because it indicates that the system has exited its stable tolerance zone. This visual structure matters because it clarifies that thresholds are not arbitrary alarm points. They are the defined limits of absorbable variation, and crossing them initiates action because the system has moved beyond the bounds within which passive continuity remains acceptable.

Threshold breaches therefore represent meaningful deviation, but they are not equivalent to collapse. A breach indicates that the system is no longer operating within stable limits. It does not indicate that the system has already failed. This distinction is essential because the purpose of the mechanism is preventive adjustment, not post-failure recognition. If threshold breach were treated as synonymous with failure, the mechanism would activate too late. The value of the threshold is that it identifies the point at which response becomes necessary before instability fully emerges.

This gives threshold breaches a specific structural meaning. Within tolerance bands, variation is being absorbed by existing system configuration. Beyond the threshold, the same system configuration is no longer sufficient to maintain alignment without intervention. The system may continue to function after the breach. Income may still be arriving. Expenses may still be paid. Liquidity may still be present. Exposure may not yet have produced visible stress. But the system's operating position has moved outside the range within which these conditions remain reliably stable. The breach signals that continued passive operation is no longer appropriate.

Triggers convert this condition into action. A trigger is not simply awareness that a threshold has been crossed. It is the defined condition under which the system initiates response. This means triggers must be structured so that action occurs at the right time and with the right relationship to the underlying signal. If triggers are too weak, threshold breaches are observed but not acted upon, allowing deviation to persist. If triggers are too sensitive, the system reacts to movement that should still be absorbed, undermining stability through unnecessary adjustment. The trigger therefore regulates response timing and response discipline.

The need for structured triggers follows directly from the difference between detection and intervention. A system may know that a signal has moved beyond its threshold and still fail to act coherently unless the trigger condition is defined. The trigger answers the practical question that the threshold alone does not answer: when does recognized deviation become mandatory for response? In a functioning governance structure, the trigger closes the gap between evaluation and adjustment. It ensures that threshold breach is not merely registered but operationalized.

The mechanism also clarifies that system behavior changes once thresholds are breached. Within tolerance bands, variation is absorbed.

The system remains within a range where ordinary movement can be contained without disproportionate consequence. Beyond thresholds, this changes. The same class of variation begins to produce larger effects because the system is no longer operating with the same margin. Liquidity that was sufficient inside the band may become constraining outside it. Expense variation that was previously neutral may begin to compress capacity materially. Income timing changes that were once manageable may now produce direct pressure. Exposure shifts that were tolerable within limits may become destabilizing once concentration exceeds the acceptable range.

This is the non-linear property of threshold behavior. Stability does not deteriorate at a constant rate as limits are exceeded. Consequences accelerate because the system has moved from a zone of absorption into a zone of transmission. Inside the band, deviation is dampened. Outside the band, deviation is amplified. This is why thresholds matter. They do not merely label change. They mark the point at which system behavior itself changes. Once crossed, the same magnitude of variation can no longer be assumed to have the same effect.

The stability implication follows directly. Stability depends on properly defined thresholds and properly structured triggers. A system without thresholds cannot distinguish absorbable variation from meaningful deviation. A system without triggers cannot convert recognized deviation into timely response. In the first case, the system drifts because it lacks limits. In the second case, the system delays because it lacks activation structure. Both conditions degrade control.

A system can also fail through miscalibration. If thresholds are too broad, meaningful deviation remains classified as acceptable variation. The system delays response until misalignment has become more severe than necessary. If thresholds are too narrow, routine movement is repeatedly treated as actionable, creating excessive intervention. If triggers are unreliable, the system responds inconsistently to similar conditions, reducing coherence in control. Effective governance therefore requires that limits correspond to actual system behavior rather than to arbitrary preference or isolated observation. Thresholds must separate what the system can absorb from what it cannot safely ignore.

The temporal progression of the mechanism clarifies how this structure develops. In the early stage, thresholds are undefined or too broad. The system has some awareness of variation, but the limits that separate normal movement from actionable deviation are either absent or insufficiently calibrated. Most variation is treated as acceptable, including changes that should already be understood as meaningful. Because thresholds are weak or missing, triggers do not activate with consistency. Action is delayed not because deviation is invisible, but because the system lacks a defined boundary for when that deviation becomes actionable.

This stage is characterized by permissiveness. Variation accumulates under the assumption that the system remains within acceptable conditions, even when meaningful deviation is already forming. The result is underresponse. The system continues to operate, but it does so without structured limits, allowing alignment to weaken before action is initiated.

In the mid stage, thresholds exist, but triggers are applied inconsistently. The system has developed some structure for identifying acceptable variation and meaningful deviation. Stability bands are more clearly defined, and breaches can be recognized. However, response remains uneven. Some signals crossing thresholds prompt action, while others are ignored, delayed, or treated ambiguously. The mechanism is present, but it is not fully reliable.

This stage is characterized by inconsistency rather than absence. The system sometimes acts appropriately and sometimes fails to respond when the same logic would require intervention. As a result, control is improved relative to the early stage but remains incomplete. The system avoids some accumulation of misalignment, yet still allows threshold breaches to persist without timely correction. Stability depends not only on having limits, but on applying them consistently.

In the late stage, thresholds are calibrated to actual system behavior and triggers operate reliably. The system distinguishes between ordinary variation and meaningful deviation with sufficient precision to avoid both overreaction and underreaction. Signals crossing defined limits are consistently converted into action. The control loop becomes structurally disciplined because its decision interface is functioning as intended. Measurement feeds evaluation, evaluation compares system position to defined ranges, and triggers initiate response when those ranges are breached.

This stage is characterized by structured response. The system is not reacting continuously, but it is reacting conditionally with consistency. Variation within tolerance is absorbed. Deviation beyond threshold is addressed. Because thresholds are aligned with the system's real operating limits, and triggers are tied to those limits, adjustment occurs early enough to preserve alignment without becoming arbitrary or excessive. Stability is maintained not by eliminating variation, but by defining when variation stops being acceptable and must be corrected.

The boundary condition of the mechanism is absence or miscalibration of thresholds and triggers. Without defined limits, the system cannot determine when to act. Without reliable triggers, it cannot ensure that recognized deviation produces response. In one form, this failure appears as passivity: meaningful deviation is allowed to persist because the system has no effective boundary marking the need for adjustment. In the other form, it appears as overcorrection: routine variation is repeatedly treated as destabilizing because the system has no disciplined distinction between noise and actionable signal. Both conditions undermine stability.

The Threshold & Trigger Mechanism therefore defines the structure through which action becomes disciplined. It does not eliminate judgment, but it prevents action from becoming arbitrary. It ensures that response is tied to defined system limits rather than to continuous motion or delayed crisis. This is what allows the control loop to function coherently. Observation and evaluation alone do not preserve alignment. They must be connected to limits that specify when deviation requires intervention and to triggers that ensure intervention occurs.

Action depends on limits because response must be structured around defined thresholds rather than continuous or arbitrary intervention.

The Monitoring Frequency Mechanism

The Monitoring Frequency Mechanism defines the process through which the timing of observation is structured. A financial system does not become visible simply because it can be measured. Measurement determines what can be captured, but monitoring frequency determines when that captured information is actually observed. The distinction is structural. System activity occurs continuously, while observation occurs at discrete intervals. The mechanism establishes that stability is influenced not only by the quality of measurement, but by the alignment between how often the system is observed and how quickly it changes.

A financial system is never static. Income flows adjust as they are received, delayed, or interrupted. Expenses shift in timing, magnitude, and composition. Liquidity rises and falls with each inflow and outflow. Exposure evolves as positions accumulate or concentrate. These changes occur continuously, whether or not they are being observed. Monitoring does not influence the occurrence of change. It influences the recognition of change. The Monitoring Frequency Mechanism therefore operates at the interface between system movement and system awareness, defining how closely perceived state tracks actual state over time.

The mechanism begins with the mismatch between continuous system evolution and discrete observation. A system does not pause between observation intervals. It continues to move. Observation, however, occurs at specific points. At each observation point, the system's state is captured as it exists at that moment. Between those points, the system evolves without direct observation. This creates a sequence of snapshots rather than a continuous stream of awareness. The perceived system state is therefore a reconstruction based on intermittent sampling rather than uninterrupted visibility.

Monitoring frequency determines the spacing between these observation points. When observations occur frequently, the gap between snapshots is small, and perceived state remains closely aligned with actual state. When observations occur infrequently, the gap widens, and perceived state becomes increasingly detached from actual conditions. The mechanism establishes that detection of deviation is directly dependent on this spacing. A deviation that emerges and evolves between observation points remains undetected until the next observation occurs. The longer the interval, the longer the system can move without recognition.

This positions monitoring frequency within the control loop between measurement and evaluation. Measurement provides the raw data that can describe system state. Frequency determines when that data is accessed and interpreted. Even if measurement is accurate and signals are correctly defined, the control loop cannot function effectively if observation occurs too infrequently. The system may generate meaningful signals, but those signals will not influence control if they are not observed in time. Frequency therefore determines the temporal resolution of awareness. It governs how quickly system movement becomes visible to the processes that evaluate and adjust it.

The distinction between continuous and periodic monitoring clarifies this relationship. Continuous monitoring refers to observation that occurs at a frequency high enough to approximate real-time awareness. In practice, financial systems do not operate with true continuous monitoring. All observation occurs through discrete sampling, even when that sampling is frequent. Periodic monitoring refers to observation at defined intervals—daily, weekly, monthly, or at other structured points.

The difference between these forms is not absolute but relative. A system that appears continuously monitored is one in which the sampling interval is short relative to the rate of system change.

This reveals an important constraint. Monitoring is always periodic in structure, even when perceived as continuous. The system is sampled, not continuously observed. The effectiveness of monitoring therefore depends on how the sampling interval compares to the speed of system movement. If the system changes slowly relative to the sampling interval, periodic monitoring may be sufficient. If the system changes rapidly, the same interval may be too long to capture meaningful deviation in time. The mechanism therefore defines frequency as a relative property. It cannot be evaluated in isolation. It must be evaluated in relation to system volatility.

Sampling intervals create blind spots. Between two observation points, the system continues to evolve without direct visibility. Any deviation that begins and develops within this interval is not detected until the next observation occurs. This does not prevent the system from changing. It prevents awareness of that change. The length of the sampling interval determines the size of the blind spot. Short intervals produce narrow blind spots, limiting the extent of undetected movement. Long intervals produce wide blind spots, allowing greater accumulation of deviation before detection.

The significance of blind spots is not only that they delay detection, but that they allow deviation to compound without awareness. A small change occurring early in an interval may be followed by additional changes before the system is observed again. By the time the next observation occurs, the system may have moved significantly away from its prior state. The perceived change between observations appears larger, but it represents the accumulation of multiple smaller changes that occurred within the blind spot. The system has not moved abruptly. It has moved continuously without being observed.

This creates a structural link between monitoring frequency and lag. Lag arises when awareness trails system state. Monitoring frequency determines how much of that lag is introduced by observation timing. Even with accurate measurement and correct signal definition, infrequent observation produces delayed awareness. The system may cross thresholds, generate signals, and require adjustment, but these conditions remain unrecognized until the next observation point. Frequency therefore determines how quickly the control loop can respond to emerging deviation.

Two failure modes emerge from this mechanism: under-monitoring and over-monitoring. Under-monitoring occurs when observation frequency is too low relative to the rate of system change. In this condition, sampling intervals are long, and blind spots are large. Deviation accumulates between observations, and detection occurs only after the system has already moved significantly. The control loop operates with delayed input, reducing its ability to correct misalignment early. Under-monitoring amplifies lag and allows drift to develop before it is recognized.

Over-monitoring occurs when observation frequency is too high relative to the rate of system movement. In this condition, the system is sampled more frequently than meaningful variation occurs. The result is an abundance of data points that primarily reflect noise rather than signal. Small, routine fluctuations become highly visible, increasing the likelihood that they will be interpreted as meaningful change. The control loop may then respond to variation that does not require adjustment, introducing unnecessary activity. Over-monitoring does not improve control. It distorts it by amplifying noise and increasing the difficulty of distinguishing meaningful signals.

Both conditions degrade system stability, but through different mechanisms. Under-monitoring reduces responsiveness by delaying detection. Over-monitoring reduces clarity by overwhelming the system with data that lacks meaningful variation. The Monitoring Frequency

Mechanism therefore establishes that effective observation is not defined by maximum frequency, but by appropriate frequency. The goal is not to observe as often as possible. It is to observe often enough to detect meaningful deviation without generating excessive noise.

This leads to the requirement that monitoring frequency must be matched to system volatility. Volatility, in this context, refers to the rate and magnitude of change within system components. Income that varies frequently and unpredictably requires more frequent observation than income that is stable and predictable. Expenses with high variability or timing sensitivity require closer monitoring than expenses that are stable and evenly distributed. Liquidity that fluctuates rapidly relative to obligations requires more frequent observation than liquidity that changes slowly. Exposure that is concentrated or sensitive to conditions requires closer monitoring than exposure that is broadly distributed and stable.

Uniform monitoring across all components does not satisfy this requirement. If all components are observed at the same frequency, some will be over-monitored while others are under-monitored. Stable components will produce excessive noise because they are observed more frequently than meaningful change occurs. Volatile components will produce blind spots because they are observed less frequently than their rate of change requires. Effective monitoring therefore requires differentiation. Observation frequency must be aligned with the behavior of each component relative to its impact on system stability.

This alignment improves detection by ensuring that observation intervals are short enough to capture meaningful deviation in volatile areas and long enough to avoid unnecessary noise in stable areas. The mechanism does not prescribe specific intervals. It defines the relationship that must be maintained between frequency and system movement. Observation must occur at a rate that allows deviation to be detected before it accumulates beyond manageable limits, while avoiding unnecessary sensitivity to routine variation.

The stability implication of this mechanism is that detection depends on timing. Measurement can be accurate, and thresholds can be well defined, but if observation occurs too infrequently, deviation will not be detected in time to support effective adjustment. The control loop depends on timely input. If input is delayed, evaluation and adjustment are also delayed. This allows misalignment to develop further than necessary before response occurs. Monitoring frequency therefore determines how early the system can act relative to emerging deviation.

At the same time, excessive frequency can impair stability by reducing the clarity of signals. When observation occurs too often relative to meaningful change, the system is exposed to constant variation that does not reflect structural movement. This increases the difficulty of identifying when thresholds are actually being approached or crossed. The control loop may become reactive to noise, reducing its effectiveness in maintaining alignment. Stability depends not only on detecting deviation early, but on detecting the right deviation.

The temporal progression of the Monitoring Frequency Mechanism describes how observation timing evolves relative to system behavior. In the early stage, monitoring is infrequent. Observation intervals are long relative to the rate of system change. The system is observed at widely spaced points, creating large blind spots between observations. During these intervals, deviation accumulates without detection. By the time the system is observed, the change appears significant, but it has developed gradually within the blind spot. Awareness is delayed, and adjustment occurs after misalignment has already progressed.

This stage is characterized by delayed detection. The system may be measured accurately when observed, but the timing of observation is insufficient to track system movement effectively. Control is weakened because the loop operates on outdated or incomplete representations of system state.

In the mid stage, monitoring becomes structured but remains misaligned with system volatility. Observation occurs at regular intervals, providing a consistent framework for reviewing system state. However, the frequency of observation does not match the behavior of different components. Some areas are observed too frequently, producing excessive data without meaningful variation. Others are observed too infrequently, allowing deviation to develop between observations. The system has improved visibility, but that visibility is uneven.

This stage is characterized by partial alignment. Monitoring exists and is systematic, but it is not calibrated to the system's dynamics. Detection improves relative to the early stage, but blind spots and noise remain. Control becomes more effective, but still limited by mismatches between observation timing and system movement.

In the late stage, monitoring frequency is aligned with system behavior. Observation intervals are calibrated to the volatility of different components. High-variability elements are observed frequently enough to detect meaningful deviation early. Stable elements are observed at intervals that avoid unnecessary noise while still capturing relevant change. The system maintains a balanced level of visibility, minimizing blind spots while avoiding overexposure to routine variation.

This stage is characterized by calibrated detection. The system is observed often enough to maintain alignment without being overwhelmed by noise. The control loop operates with timely and relevant input, allowing evaluation and adjustment to occur before deviation accumulates into structural misalignment. Monitoring frequency supports effective control by aligning observation timing with the pace of system change.

The boundary condition of the mechanism is mismatch between monitoring frequency and system volatility. When observation occurs too infrequently, lag increases and drift is allowed to accumulate before detection. When observation occurs too frequently, noise is amplified and signal clarity is reduced. In both cases, the control loop is degraded because its input layer does not reflect system movement accurately or usefully.

The Monitoring Frequency Mechanism therefore defines how awareness is timed relative to change. It establishes that detection is not only a function of what is measured, but of when it is observed. A system may generate accurate data and meaningful signals, but without appropriate observation timing, those signals cannot support effective control. Stability depends on the ability to detect deviation at the right time—early enough to act, but not so frequently that noise obscures meaning.

Detection depends on timing because awareness of deviation is determined by how often the system is observed relative to how quickly it changes.

The Deviation Detection Mechanism

The Deviation Detection Mechanism defines the process through which observed variation is classified as meaningful deviation from alignment. Detection is not equivalent to observation. Observation captures change as it occurs within the system. Detection interprets that change relative to system position. A financial system produces continuous variation across income, expenses, liquidity, and exposure. Observation makes that variation visible. Detection determines whether that variation represents movement away from stable alignment or remains within the bounds of normal operation.

This distinction establishes detection as an interpretive process rather than a descriptive one. A system can observe change without detecting deviation. It can register movement in balances, flows, and relationships without determining whether that movement is structurally relevant. Detection begins only when variation is evaluated against the system's current configuration to determine whether alignment has been altered. Without this step, the control loop receives signals without classification, and response becomes either indiscriminate or delayed.

The operation of the Deviation Detection Mechanism begins with the recognition that systems generate signals continuously. Signals emerge from measurement when variation exceeds normal noise thresholds and reflects potential change in system position. However, the presence of a signal does not guarantee the presence of meaningful deviation. A signal indicates that variation has occurred beyond ordinary fluctuation. Detection determines whether that variation changes the relationships that define stability. This requires a second layer of interpretation beyond signal identification.

Detection therefore sits between signal formation and threshold evaluation. Signals indicate where attention is required. Detection determines whether that attention corresponds to structural movement or temporary variation. Only after this classification can the system evaluate whether thresholds have been approached or breached. Without detection, thresholds operate on unfiltered signals, increasing the likelihood of inappropriate response. The mechanism ensures that signals are not treated as equivalent to deviation. It requires classification before action.

The classification of meaningful change is central to this mechanism. Not all variation that produces a signal alters system alignment. A change in income timing may exceed normal fluctuation without affecting overall capacity relative to load. A temporary increase in expenses may appear significant in isolation but resolve without altering baseline structure. A reduction in liquidity may occur within a range that still preserves sufficient temporal coverage. Exposure may shift within limits that do not materially change system sensitivity. Detection must distinguish between variation that affects these relationships and variation that does not.

Meaningful change is therefore defined by its impact on system relationships. A deviation is meaningful when it alters the balance between capacity and load, the proportionality between liquidity and obligation, or the distribution of exposure relative to tolerance. These relationships define alignment. Variation that leaves them intact does not constitute deviation, even if it produces a visible signal. Variation that alters them constitutes deviation, even if it appears modest in absolute terms. Detection requires evaluating variation in terms of relational impact rather than isolated magnitude.

This evaluation leads to the distinction between temporary and structural deviation. Temporary deviation refers to variation that resolves without altering the system's underlying relationships. It may produce short-term fluctuation, but it does not persist or compound in a way that changes alignment. Structural deviation refers to variation that persists, accumulates, or compounds, resulting in a shift in system relationships. It changes how capacity relates to load, how liquidity supports obligations, or how exposure affects sensitivity. The mechanism requires that detected variation be classified along this dimension.

Temporary deviation is characterized by self-resolution. The system returns to its prior configuration without requiring adjustment. The variation may have been visible and even significant in magnitude, but its duration is limited, and its effect on relationships is transient. Structural deviation is characterized by persistence or accumulation. The system does not return to its prior configuration. Instead, the variation becomes embedded in the operating baseline or continues to develop over time. This persistence alters the system's structural position.

The distinction between these two forms of deviation cannot be made based on presence alone. It requires evaluation over time. A variation that appears temporary at one point may become structural if it persists or recurs. A variation that appears large may be temporary if it resolves quickly without altering relationships. Detection therefore depends not only on identifying variation, but on assessing its behavior across time. This introduces the relationship between magnitude and duration.

Magnitude alone does not determine whether deviation is meaningful. A large deviation that resolves quickly may not alter system alignment. A small deviation that persists over multiple periods may accumulate into a structural change. The mechanism establishes that both magnitude and duration must be evaluated together. Magnitude indicates the size of variation at a given point. Duration indicates whether that variation persists or compounds. Detection requires integrating these dimensions to determine whether the system is experiencing temporary fluctuation or structural movement.

This integration prevents misinterpretation of isolated observations. A system that evaluates variation based solely on magnitude may overreact to large but temporary changes. A system that evaluates variation based solely on persistence may underreact to large changes that immediately alter relationships. Detection requires recognizing when magnitude is sufficient to produce immediate structural impact and when duration converts small variation into meaningful deviation over time. The mechanism therefore operates on a combined assessment of size and persistence rather than on either dimension alone.

Misclassification arises when this assessment fails. Two primary errors define this failure. The first is treating temporary variation as structural deviation. In this case, the system interprets short-term fluctuation as meaningful change and initiates adjustment unnecessarily. This produces overreaction. The control loop responds to variation that would have resolved without intervention, potentially introducing instability through unnecessary recalibration. The second error is treating structural deviation as temporary variation. In this case, the system assumes that persistent or compounding change will resolve on its own and delays adjustment. This produces underreaction. Misalignment accumulates because the system fails to respond to meaningful deviation.

Both errors distort control, but in different ways. Overreaction introduces volatility into the system by repeatedly adjusting in response to noise or temporary fluctuation. Underreaction allows drift to accumulate by delaying response to structural change. The Deviation Detection Mechanism exists to prevent both outcomes by ensuring that classification of variation is aligned with its actual impact on system relationships. Accurate detection stabilizes the control loop by aligning response with the nature of deviation.

The interaction between detection and other system mechanisms clarifies its role. Measurement provides data, and signal formation identifies variation that exceeds normal noise. Detection evaluates whether that variation constitutes meaningful deviation. Thresholds then determine whether the detected deviation requires action. Monitoring frequency determines when variation is observed, influencing how quickly detection can occur. The Deviation Detection Mechanism therefore does not replace these processes. It connects them by ensuring that signals are interpreted correctly before thresholds and triggers are applied.

Without detection, the control loop operates on unclassified input. Signals are treated as equivalent, and response becomes either excessive or insufficient. With detection, the control loop operates on structured input. Signals are classified according to their impact on alignment, allowing thresholds and triggers to function as intended. The mechanism therefore enables the transition from observation to action by providing the interpretive layer that distinguishes meaningful deviation from routine variation.

The stability implication is that accurate classification of deviation is necessary for maintaining alignment. A system can measure accurately, detect signals correctly, define thresholds appropriately, and observe at suitable frequency, yet still fail if it cannot classify variation correctly. Stability depends on responding to the right changes and ignoring those that do not affect alignment. Detection ensures that response is directed at structural movement rather than at noise or temporary fluctuation.

The temporal progression of the mechanism describes how classification develops over time. In the early stage, detection is undifferentiated. The system observes variation and may even identify signals, but it lacks the ability to distinguish between temporary and structural deviation. All variation is treated similarly, or classification is applied inconsistently without a clear framework. The system may react to visible change without understanding its significance, or it may ignore variation that later proves to be structurally important. Detection exists in a basic form, but it does not provide reliable guidance for response.

This stage is characterized by lack of discrimination. The system sees change but does not interpret it effectively. Control is weakened because response is not aligned with the nature of deviation. The system alternates between overreaction and underreaction without a consistent basis for distinguishing between them.

In the mid stage, partial classification emerges. The system begins to differentiate between temporary and structural deviation, but this differentiation is incomplete or inconsistent. Some variations are correctly identified as transient and allowed to resolve without intervention. Others are correctly identified as persistent and addressed. However, misclassification still occurs. The system may correctly classify deviation in some cases and fail in others, particularly when variation is ambiguous in magnitude or duration.

This stage is characterized by developing but imperfect interpretation. Detection improves, but it remains sensitive to error. The control loop becomes more effective because some responses are aligned with actual system movement, but instability persists where misclassification occurs. The system has a framework for detection, but it has not yet achieved reliability in applying that framework.

In the late stage, detection becomes accurate and consistent. The system reliably distinguishes between temporary variation and structural deviation. Signals are evaluated in terms of their impact on system relationships, and magnitude and duration are integrated into classification. Temporary fluctuations are allowed to resolve without unnecessary adjustment. Structural deviations are identified early enough to be addressed before they accumulate into larger misalignment. Detection supports stable control by ensuring that response corresponds to actual system movement.

This stage is characterized by alignment between variation and interpretation. The system no longer treats all signals equally. It applies classification consistently, allowing the control loop to function with precision. Stability is maintained because the system responds to meaningful change while avoiding unnecessary reaction to noise or transient fluctuation.

The boundary condition of the Deviation Detection Mechanism is persistent misclassification. When the system consistently misinterprets variation, either by overclassifying temporary fluctuation as structural or underclassifying structural movement as temporary, control is degraded. Overclassification produces excessive adjustment, introducing instability through unnecessary change. Underclassification delays response, allowing misalignment to accumulate. In both cases, the system fails to maintain alignment because its interpretation of deviation does not correspond to actual system behavior.

Failure in this mechanism does not require absence of detection. It occurs when detection exists but is inaccurate. The system may observe variation, identify signals, and apply classification, but if that classification is consistently incorrect, the control loop cannot maintain stability. The mechanism therefore defines not only the presence of detection, but the accuracy of classification as the critical factor in effective governance.

The Deviation Detection Mechanism establishes that detection is the point at which variation becomes meaningful within the control process. It transforms observed change into classified deviation, providing the basis for evaluating whether and how the system should respond. Without this transformation, the system cannot distinguish between movement that matters and movement that does not. With it, the system gains the ability to align response with actual structural change.

Detection enables response because accurate identification of deviation is required before thresholds and triggers can function effectively.

The Adjustment Mechanism

The Adjustment Mechanism defines the process through which detected and classified deviation is corrected by modifying system components or the relationships between them. A financial system does not maintain stability through observation alone. Measurement, signal formation, detection, thresholds, and triggers establish awareness and determine when action is required. Adjustment is the point at which that awareness is translated into change. It is the execution layer of the control loop. Without it, the system can identify misalignment but cannot influence its own trajectory.

Adjustment operates by altering the configuration of the system in response to deviation. When variation has been classified as structurally meaningful and threshold conditions have been met, the system must modify its state to restore alignment. This modification does not occur abstractly. It occurs through changes in income behavior, expense structure, liquidity positioning, or exposure distribution. These are the domains through which the system exists. Adjustment therefore acts directly on these domains, not on the signal or the detection itself. The signal identifies the condition. Adjustment changes the condition.

This establishes adjustment as a forward-moving process rather than a reactive one. It is not limited to responding to the current state. It alters the path the system will follow. When a deviation is left uncorrected, the system continues along a trajectory defined by that deviation. When adjustment is applied, the trajectory is changed. The system is redirected toward a configuration in which relationships are restored within stable bounds. The mechanism therefore operates on the future behavior of the system as much as on its present condition.

Within the control loop, the Adjustment Mechanism occupies the output stage. Measurement provides input, detection classifies variation, and thresholds determine when deviation requires response. Adjustment is the response. It is the point at which the system exerts influence over itself. Without this stage, the control loop remains informational. It observes and evaluates but does not act. With adjustment, the loop becomes functional. It not only interprets system state but actively maintains alignment by modifying that state.

The mechanism operates through four primary domains of intervention: income, expenses, liquidity, and exposure. These domains define the structure of the system. Adjustment occurs by modifying one or more of them to restore the relationships that define stability. Income adjustments alter the magnitude, timing, or reliability of inflow. Expense adjustments modify the level, structure, or sequencing of system load. Liquidity adjustments change buffer levels, accessibility, or allocation relative to obligations. Exposure adjustments redistribute or reduce concentration and sensitivity across the system. All corrective action must occur within these domains because they are the components through which alignment is expressed.

Each domain represents a different pathway for altering system relationships. A deviation in capacity relative to load may be addressed by increasing inflow, reducing load, or adjusting liquidity to extend temporal coverage. A deviation in timing alignment may be addressed by altering the sequencing of inflow and outflow or by adjusting buffers to absorb mismatch. A deviation in exposure may be addressed by redistributing dependency across sources or reducing concentration in a single channel. The mechanism does not prioritize one domain over another. It defines the available dimensions along which adjustment can occur.

The scale of adjustment determines the magnitude of change applied to the system. Scale must correspond to the degree of misalignment. A minor deviation that slightly alters system relationships requires limited correction. A significant deviation that materially changes capacity, load, or exposure requires a larger intervention. The mechanism establishes that scale is not arbitrary. It is proportional. Adjustment that is too small relative to the deviation will fail to restore alignment. Adjustment that is too large may overshoot, introducing new misalignment in the opposite direction.

Scale also interacts with timing. A deviation that is addressed early may require only incremental adjustment because it has not yet accumulated. The same deviation, if left uncorrected, may require a larger intervention because it has compounded over time. The mechanism therefore links scale to both magnitude and duration of deviation. Adjustment must match not only the size of the misalignment at a given moment but the extent to which that misalignment has been allowed to develop.

This leads to the distinction between incremental and large corrections. Incremental adjustment consists of small, continuous modifications applied over time to maintain alignment. It operates by preventing deviation from accumulating. When applied consistently, incremental correction keeps the system within stable bounds without requiring significant disruption. Large correction consists of substantial, discrete change applied to restore alignment after deviation has progressed beyond manageable limits. It operates by resetting system relationships more abruptly.

Each form of correction has a different effect on system stability. Incremental adjustment maintains continuity by distributing correction across time. It minimizes disruption because each change is small relative to the system's overall structure. However, it depends on early detection and timely application. If deviation is not identified early, incremental adjustment may be insufficient to restore alignment. Large correction restores alignment more quickly when misalignment has become significant. However, it introduces greater disruption because it alters system configuration more abruptly. The mechanism therefore does not favor one form exclusively. It establishes that the appropriate form depends on the state of the system at the point of intervention.

Adjustment also produces secondary effects because system components are interconnected. A change applied within one domain alters relationships in others. An adjustment to expenses reduces system load, but also affects liquidity accumulation and the balance between inflow and outflow. An adjustment to income increases capacity, but may alter exposure if that increase depends on a concentrated source. A change in liquidity affects the system's ability to absorb variation and alters the timing relationship between resources and obligations. An adjustment to exposure redistributes dependency, affecting both capacity and sensitivity.

These interactions mean that adjustment cannot be evaluated in isolation. A correction that resolves one aspect of misalignment may introduce change elsewhere in the system. The mechanism requires that adjustment account for these interactions. It is not sufficient to modify a single component without considering its effect on the overall configuration. Effective adjustment restores alignment across relationships rather than correcting one variable while destabilizing another.

The presence of secondary effects does not prevent adjustment. It defines its complexity. The system must consider how changes propagate through interconnected components. This does not introduce new mechanisms. It reflects the structural property that all system components operate within a shared configuration. Adjustment therefore requires coherence. Changes must be applied in a way that aligns relationships collectively rather than shifting misalignment from one domain to another.

The stability implication of the Adjustment Mechanism is that stability depends not only on identifying deviation, but on correcting it appropriately. Detection without adjustment leaves the system unchanged. Adjustment that is misaligned with the nature of the deviation can worsen the condition it is intended to resolve. Stability is maintained when correction restores relationships within stable bounds without introducing new forms of imbalance. This requires that adjustment be proportional, timely, and coordinated across system components.

Improper adjustment introduces a distinct form of instability. If correction is insufficient, misalignment persists. The system remains outside stable bounds, and deviation continues to influence system behavior. If correction is excessive, the system may overshoot, creating new deviation in the opposite direction. If correction is poorly coordinated, secondary effects may produce new imbalances that require further adjustment. In each case, the system fails not because it lacked awareness, but because execution did not align with the nature of the deviation.

The temporal progression of the mechanism describes how adjustment evolves as a control function. In the early stage, adjustment is reactive and inconsistent. Corrections occur after deviation has already progressed and are applied without a consistent relationship to system state. The system may respond to visible misalignment, but the response is delayed and not calibrated to the underlying condition. Adjustments may be too large or too small relative to the deviation, and secondary effects may not be considered. Control exists, but it operates with low precision.

This stage is characterized by instability in execution. The system acts, but its actions are not consistently aligned with the structure of the problem. Correction may temporarily improve conditions, but misalignment persists because adjustment is not proportional or coordinated. The system oscillates between undercorrection and overcorrection.

In the mid stage, adjustment becomes more structured but remains imperfect. The system applies corrections with greater consistency and begins to align scale with the degree of deviation. Incremental and large corrections are used with some differentiation. However, timing may still lag behind system movement, and secondary effects may not be fully integrated into the adjustment process. The system improves its ability to restore alignment, but it does not yet do so reliably.

This stage is characterized by partial calibration. The system's adjustments are more coherent, but still subject to error in scale, timing, or coordination. Misalignment is addressed more effectively than in the early stage, but inefficiencies remain. The system may require multiple adjustments to achieve alignment because initial corrections do not fully resolve the deviation or introduce new effects that require additional intervention.

In the late stage, adjustment becomes calibrated and integrated. Corrections are applied in proportion to the magnitude and duration of deviation. Timing aligns with detection, allowing intervention before misalignment accumulates. Incremental adjustments are used to maintain alignment continuously, while larger corrections are applied when necessary to restore structure. Secondary effects are accounted for, and changes are coordinated across system components. The system modifies its trajectory with precision, maintaining alignment without introducing instability.

This stage is characterized by controlled execution. Adjustment functions as an effective output of the control loop, translating evaluation into system change in a consistent and proportional manner. Stability is maintained not by avoiding variation, but by correcting it in a way that preserves system relationships.

The boundary condition of the Adjustment Mechanism is misaligned correction. Failure occurs when adjustment is insufficient, excessive, or poorly coordinated. Insufficient adjustment leaves the system outside stable bounds, allowing deviation to persist. Excessive adjustment creates new imbalance by overshooting the required correction. Poor coordination introduces secondary effects that destabilize other components. In each case, the system's trajectory is altered in a way that does not restore alignment.

This form of failure highlights the distinction between awareness and execution. A system may detect deviation accurately and determine that action is required, yet still fail if the adjustment applied does not correspond to the nature of the deviation. The mechanism therefore defines execution as a distinct requirement of stability. It is not enough to know when to act. The system must apply correction in a way that restores alignment without introducing additional instability.

The Adjustment Mechanism completes the control loop by converting evaluation into change. It ensures that detected deviation does not remain as a static condition, but becomes the basis for modifying system behavior. Through this process, the system maintains alignment over time, not by eliminating variation, but by continuously correcting it.

Correction changes trajectory because adjustment alters the system's path, determining whether deviation is reduced or allowed to continue.

The Overcorrection Mechanism

The Overcorrection Mechanism defines the process through which adjustments that exceed the scale, timing, or coordination required to restore alignment introduce new instability into the system. Adjustment is necessary because detected deviation does not correct itself. A financial system that has moved outside stable bounds must be altered if alignment is to be restored. But the existence of correction as a stabilizing function does not mean that every correction is stabilizing in effect. A system does not lose stability only when control is absent. It can also lose stability when control is present but miscalibrated. In that condition, instability is not produced by neglect. It is produced by intervention.

This mechanism begins from a distinction established in the prior chapter. Adjustment changes system trajectory. It alters the path the system will follow by modifying income, expenses, liquidity, exposure, or the relationships between them. When adjustment is proportional, timely, and coordinated, that trajectory moves back toward stable alignment. When adjustment exceeds what is required, the trajectory does not settle into alignment. It passes through it. The system is not merely corrected. It is displaced beyond the point of stability into a new form of misalignment. Overcorrection therefore does not represent failure to act. It represents action that distorts the system beyond what restoration requires.

The consequence is structural. The system becomes unstable because of how it is corrected. That instability is not external to the control process. It is generated within it. A deviation is detected, classified, and evaluated against thresholds. A response is initiated with the intention of restoring stable relationships. But if the scale of the response is too large, if the timing of the response is too abrupt or too delayed relative to current state, or if the correction is not coordinated across interacting components, the intervention itself creates a new deviation. The system is then forced into another round of correction, not because the original deviation remains unchanged, but because the corrective process has produced a new imbalance.

The mechanism operates in a clear sequence. First, deviation is detected. A signal is measured, interpreted, and classified as meaningful movement away from alignment. A threshold is breached, and the system determines that passive absorption is no longer sufficient. Second, adjustment is applied. The control loop initiates a change intended to restore the relationships that define stability. Third, the adjustment exceeds requirement. Its scale is too large relative to the size of the deviation, its timing does not match the state the system is actually in when the response takes effect, or its coordination is incomplete, so that changes in one domain distort relationships elsewhere. Fourth, the system overshoots alignment. Instead of settling within stable range, it moves beyond that range in the opposite direction. Fifth, the overshoot becomes a new deviation. The system is now misaligned again, but not in the original form. Sixth, this new deviation generates another signal and another adjustment. The loop does not converge. It begins to oscillate.

Oscillation is the primary expression of the Overcorrection Mechanism. The system moves from aligned to misaligned, then through correction past alignment into opposite-direction misalignment, and then back again through further attempts at restoration. This is not random instability. It is structured instability created by the control process itself. The movement is patterned. It emerges because each response is large enough, abrupt enough, or poorly integrated enough to cross through the stable range rather than settling into it. Instead of reducing deviation toward equilibrium, the control loop generates repeated motion around equilibrium without reaching it.

This pattern reveals why overcorrection is distinct from both drift and uncorrected deviation. Drift is gradual movement away from alignment under insufficient control. Overcorrection is repeated movement through and beyond alignment under miscalibrated control. Drift reflects passivity. Overcorrection reflects excessive or distorted intervention. In both cases, the system loses stability, but the causal pathway is different. The Overcorrection Mechanism therefore identifies a specific control failure: instability created not by failure to respond, but by responding beyond requirement.

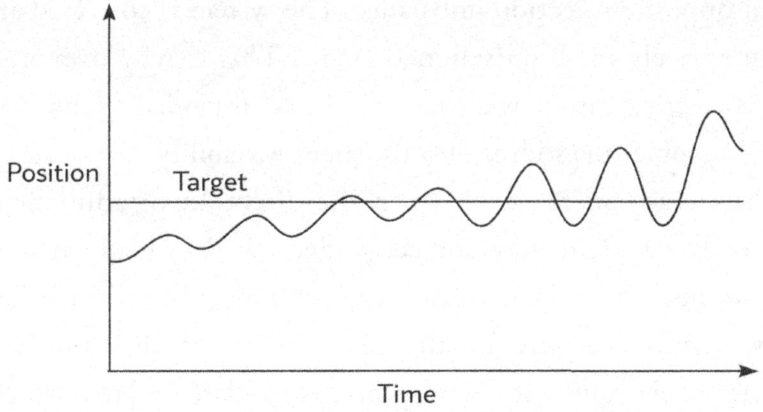

[Figure 6: Oscillation from Overcorrection]

The figure represents this process as repeated movement across the stable range rather than convergence into it. The system begins with deviation from alignment, but the corrective action moves it past the equilibrium zone instead of into it. That overshoot becomes the basis for the next corrective response, which again crosses the alignment point in the opposite direction. The pattern is oscillatory because each act of correction generates the conditions for the next deviation. Stability is not absent because nothing is happening. It is absent because too much is happening in the wrong proportion. The increasing or persistent swings shown in the figure indicate that the system is being destabilized by the structure of its own control process.

Overshoot is the direct mechanism through which this occurs. Overshoot means that adjustment exceeds the amount required to restore alignment. The system does not stop at stable range. It crosses through it. A small deviation combined with a large correction produces a large displacement. The effect is not merely that the original problem is removed. It is that the response creates an opposite-direction imbalance. The system is corrected and then immediately made misaligned again. This is why overshoot converts correction into new deviation. The act intended to eliminate instability becomes the source of subsequent instability.

Overshoot can emerge even when the direction of adjustment is correct. The system may correctly identify that load must be reduced, liquidity must be increased, exposure must be redistributed, or inflow conditions must be altered. But correct direction does not ensure stable result. If the response is too large relative to the deviation, the correction does not restore proportionality. It replaces one disproportion with another. Stability depends not only on moving in the right direction, but on moving by the right amount.

Feedback amplification develops from this point. A control loop ordinarily stabilizes because feedback allows the system to compare current position to desired position and reduce the gap. Under overcorrection, the loop continues to respond, but the object of response changes. The system is no longer reacting only to the original deviation. It is reacting to the effects of its prior correction. The sequence becomes self-reinforcing. Deviation leads to correction. Correction leads to overshoot. Overshoot generates a new signal. That signal leads to further correction. The loop now amplifies variation instead of reducing it.

This inversion is structurally important. Feedback is not inherently stabilizing. It is stabilizing only when the relationship between signal and response is calibrated to system behavior. When that calibration fails, the same feedback architecture that should preserve alignment begins to generate volatility. The loop is still functioning in a formal sense. Signals are still being detected. Thresholds are still being crossed. Adjustments are still being made. But the effect of those adjustments is no longer convergence. It is amplification. This is why overcorrection must be understood as a control failure rather than as an absence of control. The system is being managed, but the management process is producing instability.

This creates the key inversion of the mechanism. Instability is not coming from external shock. It is not coming from passive drift. It is coming from the intervention process itself. The system may, in fact, have been more stable with a smaller correction, a slower correction, a more coordinated correction, or no correction at the magnitude that was actually applied. Control introduces volatility when misapplied. This does not mean correction is undesirable. It means that correction must correspond to system need. Stability cannot be restored by action alone. It is restored by calibrated action.

Two drivers are central to this miscalibration: scale distortion and timing distortion. Scale distortion occurs when the size of the adjustment exceeds the size of the deviation. The response is larger than the misalignment requires. This produces overshoot directly because the system is moved farther than necessary to restore stable relationships. Timing distortion occurs when adjustment is applied too quickly relative to system absorption or too late relative to current system position. A response that is correct in direction and even reasonable in scale can still become destabilizing if it reaches the system at the wrong moment. By the time the adjustment takes effect, the system may already have changed, making the response excessive relative to current conditions.

Timing distortion is especially important in dynamic systems because system state does not remain fixed between detection and adjustment. A deviation may be identified at one point, but the system continues to evolve while response is being formulated and implemented. If the correction arrives after the system has already partially self-adjusted or shifted in other ways, the intervention may now exceed current need. Likewise, a correction applied too abruptly can produce a rate-of-change mismatch even if the total intended change is not inherently excessive. The system is displaced too quickly to settle into alignment. In both cases, timing misalignment converts potentially stabilizing action into destabilizing movement.

Coordination distortion compounds these problems. Because the system operates through linked domains, correction in one area affects relationships elsewhere. An intervention that is reasonable in one component may create imbalance in another if it is not coordinated system-wide. A reduction in one form of load may alter liquidity dynamics. A change in exposure may affect capacity sensitivity. A shift in inflow conditions may change the balance between stability and concentration. If adjustment is applied as though components were isolated, the system may overshoot relationally even when no single variable appears to overshoot in absolute terms. Overcorrection can therefore be produced not only by too much adjustment in one place, but by incomplete integration across places.

The mechanism connects directly to earlier chapters. In Chapter 7, thresholds determine when action is required. Poor threshold calibration can make triggers premature or exaggerated, initiating response before the system has actually moved far enough to require the magnitude of action taken. In Chapter 9, detection classifies deviation. Misclassification can produce the wrong form of response, treating temporary movement as structural and thereby inviting excessive correction. In Chapter 10, adjustment defines how correction is applied. Scale mismatch there becomes the direct cause of overshoot here. And in Chapter 5, the control loop is defined as the structure through which governance operates. The Overcorrection Mechanism shows that a functioning loop is not sufficient for stability. The loop must also be proportionate. Otherwise, it produces instability instead of alignment.

At the system level, overcorrection produces a distinct operating condition. Variability increases because each adjustment becomes the source of subsequent movement. Predictability declines because the system no longer settles after intervention. Continuous adjustment cycles become normal. The system appears actively managed, yet it is structurally unstable. This appearance can be misleading. Activity may be mistaken for control because the system is continually being observed and modified. But repeated intervention is not evidence of stable governance if the interventions themselves are amplifying deviation. An actively managed system can be less stable than a less active one if the management process is miscalibrated.

The stability implication follows directly. Stability requires correction, but correction must be proportional, timely, and coordinated. If deviation is ignored, drift accumulates. But if deviation is corrected excessively or without proper integration, the system loses stability through oscillation. Stability therefore depends on a middle condition: enough intervention to restore alignment, but not so much that the correction itself becomes a new source of imbalance. Without proportionality, control becomes the source of instability.

The temporal progression of the mechanism makes this clearer. In the early stage, overshoot is minor. Corrections slightly exceed requirement, producing small oscillations. The system still stabilizes over time because the displacement on either side of alignment remains limited. The control loop is imprecise, but not yet self-destabilizing in a severe way. Small swings occur, but convergence remains possible.

In the mid stage, overcorrection becomes repeated. Corrections consistently exceed requirement, and the system moves back and forth across alignment with increasing regularity. Stability becomes inconsistent because the system no longer settles quickly after intervention. Oscillation is now visible as a pattern rather than as occasional imprecision. The system remains controllable, but its control process is generating unnecessary variability.

In the late stage, instability becomes persistent. Overshoot cycles continue without convergence. Each corrective action creates the conditions for the next misalignment, and the control loop amplifies variation rather than absorbing it. The system cannot settle into stable range because its own interventions repeatedly move it beyond that range. This is control-driven instability in full form.

Failure occurs when adjustment repeatedly exceeds required scale, feedback amplification persists, and the system cannot converge to stable alignment. At that point, the system is no longer unstable because it has been left unmanaged. It is unstable because management has become the mechanism of instability. The control loop remains active, but its activity is structurally miscalibrated. The result is not restored alignment, but continuous oscillation around it.

The Overcorrection Mechanism therefore defines the limit condition of intervention itself. It shows that correction is necessary, but not self-justifying. The existence of response does not prove the presence of stable control. A system can be unstable through absence of adjustment, but it can also be unstable through excess of adjustment. What matters is whether intervention restores alignment without generating new deviation. Stability depends on correction that converges rather than correction that overshoots.

The Recalibration Mechanism

The Recalibration Mechanism defines the process through which a financial system resets its baseline configuration after deviation has altered its underlying structure. Adjustment operates within an existing frame of reference. It restores alignment relative to a baseline that is assumed to remain valid. Recalibration begins when that assumption no longer holds. The system is not misaligned relative to a stable reference. The reference itself has become outdated. In that condition, restoring alignment to the prior baseline is no longer possible. Stability can only be reestablished by redefining what alignment means.

This distinction separates recalibration from routine correction. Adjustment modifies system position within a given structure. Recalibration modifies the structure that defines position. The system does not return to its prior state. It establishes a new state from which alignment will be evaluated going forward. Stability is therefore not achieved by reversing change. It is achieved by incorporating change into a new configuration that can operate within stable bounds.

The mechanism operates when a sequence of conditions converges. Deviation is first detected and classified through the processes established in prior chapters. The system identifies that its relationships have moved outside stable range. Adjustment is then applied in an attempt to restore alignment. Under normal conditions, this would return the system to its baseline configuration. However, if the conditions that defined that baseline have changed, adjustment cannot complete its function. The system cannot reestablish prior relationships because the underlying environment or internal structure no longer supports them. The baseline becomes non-operational.

At this point, the system transitions from adjustment to recalibration. The prior baseline is no longer treated as the reference for alignment. Instead, the system redefines its baseline by establishing new relationships between income, expenses, liquidity, and exposure. These relationships determine what constitutes stable operation under current conditions. Once this new configuration is established, a new alignment range is defined. Thresholds shift, tolerance bands adjust, and expectations are repositioned. The system resumes operation, but it does so relative to a different reference point.

The concept of baseline is central to this mechanism. A baseline is the reference state against which variation is evaluated. It defines what is considered normal, acceptable, and stable. All processes within the control loop—measurement, detection, threshold evaluation, and adjustment—operate relative to this reference. If the baseline accurately reflects system conditions, alignment can be maintained through incremental correction. If the baseline becomes outdated, these processes continue to function, but they operate against an invalid frame. The system may appear to be actively correcting deviation, yet fail to achieve stability because the target of correction no longer corresponds to reality.

Recalibration resolves this mismatch by updating the definition of normal. The original baseline reflected a prior set of conditions. These conditions may have included a certain level of income reliability, a specific structure of expenses, a particular liquidity requirement, or an acceptable degree of exposure concentration. When these conditions change in a structural way, the original baseline ceases to be a valid reference. The system cannot restore alignment by returning to it. Recalibration requires redefining these expectations so that alignment can be evaluated relative to current conditions rather than past configurations.

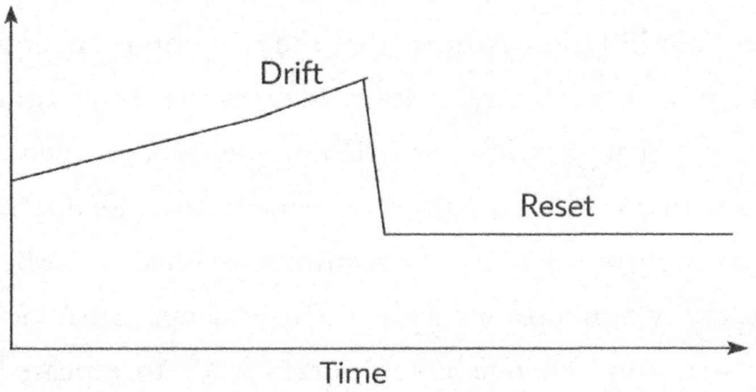

[Figure 7: Recalibration Shift Model]

The figure represents this process as a shift in the reference frame rather than a movement back toward a fixed point. The system begins with a baseline that defines its stable operating range. Deviation moves the system away from that range. Adjustment attempts to return it. When the baseline is no longer valid, repeated adjustments fail to converge. Recalibration shifts the baseline itself, creating a new stable range around the system's current configuration. Stability is restored not by reversing movement, but by repositioning the frame within which movement is evaluated.

Recalibration can take two forms: temporary and structural. Temporary recalibration involves a short-term adjustment of expectations while maintaining the assumption that the system will eventually return to its prior baseline. It represents adaptation within the same structure. The system acknowledges that conditions have changed in the short term and adjusts its evaluation accordingly, but does not redefine its long-term configuration. Structural recalibration involves a permanent change in system configuration. The prior baseline is replaced by a new one, and the system no longer treats the previous state as a valid reference. It represents replacement of structure rather than adaptation within it.

The distinction between these forms is defined by persistence. Temporary recalibration assumes that the conditions causing deviation are transient. Structural recalibration assumes that those conditions are enduring. If a change in income reliability persists, if expense structure shifts in a lasting way, if liquidity requirements increase due to sustained changes in timing or volatility, or if exposure dynamics evolve beyond prior tolerance, the system must incorporate these changes into a new baseline. Treating structural change as temporary leads to repeated attempts to restore an outdated configuration. Treating temporary variation as structural leads to unnecessary redefinition of the system. The mechanism therefore requires classification of change not only as deviation, but as a change in the validity of the baseline itself.

Recalibration is driven by the failure of assumptions. A financial system is built on implicit expectations about how its components behave. These include assumptions about the stability and timing of income, the consistency and flexibility of expenses, the adequacy and accessibility of liquidity, and the distribution and sensitivity of exposure. These assumptions define the baseline because they determine what level of variation can be absorbed without destabilizing the system. When these assumptions no longer hold, the baseline becomes misaligned with actual conditions.

For example, if income becomes less predictable, the prior baseline that assumed stable inflow is no longer valid. If expenses become more rigid or increase in baseline level, the prior configuration of load relative to capacity is no longer sustainable. If liquidity requirements change due to shifts in timing or increased variability, the prior buffer structure no longer supports stability. If exposure becomes more concentrated or more sensitive to conditions, the prior tolerance level is no longer appropriate. In each case, the system may continue to operate using its original baseline, but it will experience persistent misalignment because its expectations do not match reality.

Recalibration requires replacing these outdated assumptions. It involves redefining what constitutes sufficient income stability, acceptable expense load, adequate liquidity coverage, and tolerable exposure. This is not a process of incremental adjustment within the existing frame. It is a redefinition of the frame itself. The system acknowledges that its prior expectations are no longer valid and establishes new ones that reflect current conditions. Stability is restored because the system's structure is brought into alignment with the environment in which it operates.

Recalibration is not a singular event. It occurs as part of an iterative process. A system may reset its baseline, operate within the new configuration, encounter further deviation as conditions continue to evolve, and recalibrate again. This does not indicate failure of recalibration. It reflects the fact that systems exist within environments that change over time. The mechanism therefore defines recalibration as a recurring capability rather than a one-time adjustment. Stability is maintained through successive updates to the baseline as conditions evolve.

The interaction between recalibration and adjustment clarifies when each mechanism applies. Adjustment restores alignment relative to an existing baseline. Recalibration redefines the baseline when restoration is no longer possible. If the system continues to apply adjustment when recalibration is required, it will experience repeated failure. Each corrective attempt will move the system toward a reference point that no longer corresponds to current conditions. The system will appear to be actively correcting deviation, yet remain misaligned because its target is outdated. This produces persistent instability through repeated, unsuccessful correction cycles.

Conversely, recalibration applied prematurely introduces its own form of instability. If the system redefines its baseline in response to temporary variation, it may abandon a valid configuration unnecessarily. This creates structural change without structural need. The system may then have to adjust again to return to a prior configuration once conditions normalize. Premature recalibration therefore produces instability by replacing a valid baseline with an unnecessary one. The mechanism requires that recalibration be applied only when structural change has invalidated the existing reference.

These two failure modes—failure to recalibrate and premature recalibration—define the boundary of the mechanism. In the first case, the system remains anchored to an outdated baseline and cannot restore alignment despite repeated adjustment. In the second case, the system changes its baseline without necessity, introducing instability through unnecessary structural change. Effective recalibration occurs when the system correctly identifies when its baseline is no longer valid and replaces it with one that reflects current conditions.

The mechanism integrates directly with prior system components. In Chapter 2, drift represents accumulated deviation that may gradually move the system away from its baseline. Over time, this accumulation can become large enough to require recalibration rather than incremental correction. In Chapter 6, measurement produces the data that reveals when system behavior no longer aligns with baseline expectations. In Chapter 7, thresholds define the limits of acceptable variation. When recalibration occurs, these thresholds shift because the underlying reference has changed. In Chapter 10, adjustment attempts to restore alignment. When it fails repeatedly, it indicates that the baseline itself may no longer be valid. In Chapter 11, repeated overcorrection may signal that the system is attempting to force alignment to an outdated reference, producing oscillation instead of convergence. Recalibration resolves this by redefining the target of correction.

At the system level, recalibration produces a distinct outcome. The system stabilizes at a new equilibrium. Oscillation is reduced because adjustment now operates relative to a valid baseline. Alignment improves because expectations match current conditions. The system no longer attempts to return to a prior state that cannot be sustained. Instead, it operates within a configuration that reflects its actual environment and structure. Stability is therefore restored not by resisting change, but by incorporating it.

This outcome clarifies the role of adaptability in maintaining stability. A system that cannot recalibrate becomes rigid. It continues to evaluate itself against outdated expectations, producing persistent misalignment. A system that recalibrates appropriately remains aligned with evolving conditions. Adaptability does not eliminate the need for control. It ensures that control operates relative to a valid reference. Stability is not achieved by preserving the past configuration. It is achieved by maintaining alignment between structure and current conditions.

The temporal progression of the Recalibration Mechanism describes how this transition occurs. In the early stage, the system resists change. It attempts to maintain its prior baseline through repeated adjustment. Deviation is detected and corrected, but correction fails to restore alignment because the baseline is no longer valid. The system continues to operate against outdated assumptions, producing repeated cycles of correction without convergence. Stability is not achieved because the reference point remains misaligned with reality.

In the mid stage, partial recalibration occurs. Some assumptions are updated, and certain components of the system adjust to reflect new conditions. The system stabilizes temporarily because these changes bring portions of the structure into alignment. However, the recalibration is incomplete. Other aspects of the baseline remain unchanged, creating inconsistencies in the system's configuration. Stability improves, but remains fragile because the system has not fully redefined its reference.

In the late stage, full recalibration is achieved. The system establishes a new baseline that reflects current conditions across all core domains. Income expectations, expense structure, liquidity requirements, and exposure tolerance are aligned with reality. The system operates within a new stable range, and adjustment resumes its role as a mechanism for maintaining alignment rather than attempting to restore an outdated configuration. Stability is restored because the system's reference frame is valid.

Failure occurs when the system continues to operate against an outdated baseline or changes its baseline without structural necessity. In the first case, persistent misalignment results because correction targets an invalid reference. In the second case, instability is introduced because the system redefines its structure unnecessarily. Both outcomes reflect failure to apply recalibration appropriately. Stability requires that the system both recognize when its baseline is no longer valid and avoid redefining it when it remains applicable.

The Recalibration Mechanism completes the transition from correction to adaptation within the control framework. It establishes that stability is not only a function of maintaining alignment within a fixed structure, but of ensuring that the structure itself remains aligned with current conditions. Adjustment preserves stability when the baseline is valid. Recalibration restores stability when the baseline has changed.

Systems must adapt to remain stable because alignment depends on maintaining a baseline that reflects current conditions rather than past configurations.

The Neglect Mechanism

The Neglect Mechanism defines the process through which a financial system loses alignment when monitoring, evaluation, and adjustment are absent or insufficiently applied. The system continues to operate. Income flows, expenses are met, liquidity moves, and exposure persists. What is absent is not activity, but control. The processes that observe system state, interpret variation, and apply correction are inactive or degraded. Instability does not arise because the system is actively mismanaged. It arises because it is not managed at all.

This distinction establishes neglect as a passive failure mode. The system does not require incorrect decisions to become unstable. It requires only the absence of continuous engagement. Financial systems are not static. They evolve continuously as their components change. Without a mechanism to monitor those changes, evaluate their implications, and adjust relationships accordingly, the system does not remain in its initial configuration. It moves. That movement is not directed. It is not coordinated. It is not corrected. Over time, this unmanaged evolution produces misalignment.

The operation of the Neglect Mechanism follows a predictable sequence. Monitoring is reduced or absent. Observation becomes infrequent, irregular, or stops entirely. The entry point of the control loop is therefore disabled. System changes continue. Income fluctuates in timing or reliability, expenses shift in level or structure, liquidity expands or contracts, and exposure evolves. These changes occur regardless of whether they are observed. No evaluation occurs. Relationships between components are not assessed, and variation is not interpreted relative to alignment. No adjustment is applied. Deviation, whether temporary or structural, is not corrected. Drift accumulates. The system moves away from its prior alignment through uncoordinated change. Instability emerges. Not as a sudden event, but as the consequence of prolonged accumulation without resistance.

The absence of monitoring is the primary driver of this mechanism. Monitoring is the entry point of control because it converts system activity into observable information. Without observation, signals are not recognized. Without signals, deviation is not detected. Without detection, no evaluation occurs. The control loop is therefore inactive at its origin. The system continues to change, but those changes are not seen. This is not equivalent to stable operation. It is equivalent to unobserved operation. The distinction is critical because stability cannot be inferred from continuity of function when observation is absent.

When monitoring is removed, the system's evolution becomes opaque. Income variability may increase without recognition. Expense structure may become more rigid or expand in baseline without being evaluated. Liquidity may decline relative to load without being measured. Exposure may concentrate or become more sensitive without being detected. These changes do not require attention to occur. They occur as part of the system's normal operation. Without monitoring, they are not identified as deviation. The system therefore cannot respond. It continues to operate under the assumption that its prior configuration remains intact.

Under these conditions, drift becomes the dominant system behavior. As established earlier, drift is the accumulation of small, continuous deviations across system components. Drift does not require large shocks or discrete disruptions. It emerges from uncoordinated movement. In the presence of governance, drift is identified and corrected before it produces significant misalignment. Under neglect, drift proceeds uninterrupted.

Each small deviation is absorbed without evaluation, and each absorption becomes part of the system's new baseline. Over time, these incremental changes accumulate into a meaningful shift in system configuration.

This accumulation is not immediately visible. The system may continue to function normally. Obligations may still be met. Income may still be received. Liquidity may still be present. This creates the appearance of stability. However, alignment is not defined by function alone. It is defined by the relationships between system components. Under neglect, those relationships are not maintained. They are allowed to evolve without coordination. The system therefore becomes misaligned even while it appears to operate successfully.

Lag expands significantly in this condition. When monitoring is active, lag represents the delay between system change and awareness. Under neglect, this delay is no longer bounded by observation intervals. It extends until consequences become visible. Awareness is no longer driven by measurement. It is driven by outcome. The system is not recognized as misaligned when deviation occurs. It is recognized as misaligned when that deviation produces constraint, stress, or failure. The gap between actual system state and perceived system state therefore becomes large. The system may have moved far from alignment before that movement is detected.

This shift transforms awareness from proactive to reactive. In a governed system, monitoring identifies deviation early, allowing correction before instability emerges. Under neglect, deviation is not detected until it produces visible effects. At that point, the system is already in a constrained position. Correction becomes more difficult because the margin for adjustment has been reduced. The system is no longer operating near its stable range. It is operating near or beyond its tolerance limits.

The accumulation of deviation under neglect produces compounding instability. Small deviations persist because they are not corrected. They interact because they occur across multiple components. They compound because each deviation alters the context in which subsequent deviations occur. A slight increase in expense load reduces available capacity. Reduced capacity increases sensitivity to income variation. Increased sensitivity amplifies the impact of liquidity reduction. Each change modifies the system's response to further change. The result is not a linear progression away from alignment, but an accelerating process of misalignment.

This compounding effect reduces margin. Margin represents the distance between the system's current position and the point at which it can no longer sustain its obligations. As deviation accumulates, this distance narrows. The system becomes less tolerant to variation. Small fluctuations that would previously have been absorbed without consequence now produce pressure. The system's ability to absorb variability declines not because a single large change has occurred, but because many small changes have accumulated without correction.

Sensitivity increases as a result. The system responds more strongly to variation because its internal buffers have been reduced. Liquidity may no longer cover periods of reduced income. Expense structure may no longer allow for flexibility. Exposure may concentrate risk in ways that amplify adverse conditions. The system becomes fragile. Not because it has been subjected to a large shock, but because it has gradually lost its capacity to absorb normal variation.

The interaction with prior mechanisms clarifies the structure of this process. Drift, as defined earlier, becomes the dominant dynamic because no counteracting adjustment is applied. Lag expands because monitoring is absent, delaying awareness until outcomes force recognition. Invisible degradation persists because the system continues to function while its underlying relationships weaken. The control loop is effectively absent, as observation, evaluation, and adjustment are not actively performed. Measurement and signal formation are inactive because data is not collected or interpreted. Detection does not occur because signals are not recognized. Thresholds are not evaluated because deviation is not identified. Adjustment and recalibration are not applied because no intervention is triggered. The entire governance structure is therefore inactive, allowing the system to evolve without constraint.

At the system level, this produces a characteristic pattern. The system appears stable initially. Function continues without interruption. This creates the perception that stability has been achieved or maintained. Beneath this appearance, degradation occurs silently. Relationships between components shift in ways that are not visible through surface indicators. Margin compresses, sensitivity increases, and alignment deteriorates. Eventually, the system reaches a point where normal variation produces instability. At that point, failure becomes visible. The transition from apparent stability to instability is abrupt in perception, but gradual in cause.

This pattern explains why failure under neglect is often interpreted as sudden. The system appears to function normally until it does not. The absence of monitoring obscures the gradual accumulation of deviation. When instability emerges, it is attributed to the immediate condition rather than to the preceding period of unmanaged change. In reality, the failure is not triggered by a single event. It is the result of accumulated deviation that has reduced the system's tolerance to variation.

Failure dynamics under neglect are therefore defined by accumulation rather than by discrete disruption. The system fails when variation exceeds remaining margin. That variation may be normal. It may not represent an extraordinary condition. What has changed is not the magnitude of variation, but the system's capacity to absorb it. Because that capacity has been eroded over time, the same level of variation that was previously manageable becomes destabilizing.

The stability implication is direct. Stability cannot be maintained passively. A financial system does not remain aligned by continuing to operate. It remains aligned by being continuously observed, evaluated, and adjusted. These processes are not optional. They are structural requirements. Without them, the system defaults to unmanaged evolution. That evolution produces drift. Drift produces misalignment. Misalignment reduces margin. Reduced margin increases sensitivity. Increased sensitivity leads to instability under normal variation.

The temporal progression of the Neglect Mechanism reflects this sequence. In the early stage, the system exhibits apparent stability. Monitoring is absent or minimal, but function continues. Deviation begins, but it is not observed. The system appears unchanged because its surface indicators have not yet been affected. In the mid stage, hidden degradation develops. Drift accumulates, margin compresses, and sensitivity increases. The system continues to function, but its internal configuration becomes less stable. This change is not visible because monitoring is insufficient to detect it. In the late stage, visible instability emerges. The system encounters variation that exceeds its reduced tolerance. Failure becomes apparent. Awareness occurs, but it is delayed relative to the underlying change.

The failure condition is defined by operation without monitoring or adjustment. When the system is allowed to evolve without observation, evaluation, and correction, deviation accumulates beyond tolerance. Instability emerges as a result of this accumulation. The system does not fail because it was subjected to an unusual condition. It fails because it was not actively maintained.

The Neglect Mechanism therefore establishes the baseline requirement for governance. Control is not required only when problems are visible. It is required continuously because system conditions change continuously. The absence of visible instability does not indicate that control can be suspended. It indicates that control has been effective or that instability has not yet become visible. Removing control does not preserve stability. It removes the process that prevents misalignment from accumulating.

Neglect accelerates failure because stability requires continuous observation and adjustment, and without them, misalignment accumulates without resistance.

The Overreaction Mechanism

The Overreaction Mechanism defines the process through which short-term variation, noise-level signals, and incomplete information trigger immediate adjustment without sufficient evaluation or classification, resulting in instability through excessive responsiveness. The system responds before it understands the nature of the change. Signals are converted directly into action, bypassing the interpretive processes required to determine whether the observed variation represents meaningful deviation or routine fluctuation. Stability is not degraded by absence of response. It is degraded by response that occurs without sufficient filtering.

This mechanism is structurally distinct from overcorrection. Overcorrection occurs when the magnitude of adjustment exceeds the magnitude of deviation. Overreaction occurs when adjustment is applied too early or too frequently relative to the information required to justify that adjustment. The failure is not in scale, but in timing and frequency. The system does not wait for classification. It treats partial signals as complete information and responds as though deviation has already been confirmed. In doing so, it converts uncertainty into action, rather than resolving uncertainty before acting.

The defining characteristic of overreaction is the separation between reaction and evaluation. A governed system operates through a sequence: observation captures system activity, detection identifies potential deviation, evaluation classifies that deviation relative to alignment, and adjustment modifies system configuration. Overreaction interrupts this sequence. It compresses the process by bypassing evaluation. Observation leads directly to action. Detection is treated as sufficient justification for adjustment. The system reacts to the presence of variation without determining whether that variation is meaningful.

This compression alters the function of control. Evaluation exists to determine magnitude relevance, duration, and structural impact. Without it, signals are treated uniformly. Short-term movement is interpreted as structural change. Temporary variation is interpreted as persistent deviation. Noise is interpreted as signal. The system therefore loses the ability to discriminate between different types of change. It responds to all variation as though it requires intervention. The result is not increased control precision. It is increased control activity without corresponding accuracy.

The mechanism becomes visible in the treatment of noise. As established earlier, financial systems generate continuous variation. Some of this variation reflects meaningful changes in alignment. Much of it reflects routine fluctuation that does not alter system relationships. Measurement processes capture both. Signal formation distinguishes between them by identifying variation that exceeds noise thresholds. Overreaction collapses this distinction. Noise becomes actionable. Short-term fluctuations are misclassified as meaningful deviation, not because the system lacks measurement, but because it fails to apply sufficient evaluation to what measurement produces.

High-frequency observation intensifies this effect. As monitoring frequency increases, the system is exposed to more data points. This does not necessarily increase clarity. It increases visibility of variation. Without filtering, this variation appears as continuous change. The system perceives movement where, at lower frequency, patterns would resolve into stable ranges. Overreaction converts this increased visibility into increased intervention. Each observed fluctuation becomes a candidate for adjustment. The system therefore begins to respond to the natural variability of its own operation.

This produces a shift in control input. Instead of acting on structured signals that represent meaningful deviation, the system acts on raw variation. Temporary fluctuations, normal variability, and non-structural movement become drivers of adjustment. The control loop is still active, but its inputs are no longer filtered. It operates on data that has not been sufficiently interpreted. This does not improve responsiveness. It degrades alignment by introducing adjustments that are not required by the system's actual position.

Instability emerges from the speed and frequency of these adjustments. When the system reacts too quickly, it does not allow time for variation to resolve or for patterns to emerge. When it reacts too frequently, it modifies its configuration continuously without allowing those modifications to stabilize. The system becomes subject to constant change. Income structure may be altered repeatedly in response to short-term variability. Expense control may be tightened and loosened in rapid succession. Liquidity positioning may shift continuously without establishing a stable buffer. Exposure distribution may be adjusted in response to transient conditions rather than persistent risk.

The consequence is that the system never stabilizes between adjustments. Each intervention changes the system's state. That new state is then immediately observed and treated as input for further reaction. Because evaluation is bypassed, the system does not distinguish between changes caused by its own prior adjustments and changes originating from underlying conditions. The system therefore reacts to the effects of its own activity. Adjustment becomes both the cause and the response to variation.

This dynamic distorts the feedback loop. In a structured control process, feedback reflects the system's position relative to alignment. Under overreaction, feedback increasingly reflects the system's prior responses. The loop compresses into a sequence of observation and reaction without sufficient separation for evaluation. The cycle becomes: observe, react, observe, react. Each observation captures a system state that has been modified by recent intervention. Each reaction modifies the system again before its behavior under the previous change can be understood. The loop does not converge toward alignment. It circulates around its own activity.

This compression reduces signal clarity. Because the system is continuously changing, it becomes difficult to distinguish between underlying variation and variation introduced by prior adjustments. Signals lose their interpretive value because they no longer represent stable relationships. The system is in motion too frequently for patterns to form. Evaluation becomes increasingly unreliable because the conditions it attempts to assess are constantly shifting. Overreaction therefore degrades not only stability, but also the system's ability to understand its own state. Because responses are driven by unclassified variation, decision outputs lose consistency relative to actual system conditions.

At the system level, the consequences are cumulative. Volatility increases because adjustments are applied in response to short-term variation rather than structural change. Predictability declines because the system's configuration is not allowed to stabilize. The baseline becomes unstable because it is repeatedly modified in response to transient conditions. The system is no longer anchored to a consistent reference point. Instead, it moves continuously in response to each observed fluctuation. Control activity increases, but alignment decreases.

This produces a characteristic condition. The system appears highly responsive. It is actively monitored, and changes are addressed immediately. However, this responsiveness does not translate into stability. It produces continuous movement without convergence. The system is not lacking control. It is dominated by it. Control activity becomes excessive relative to the information required to justify that activity. The result is instability generated by the structure of response itself.

The distinction from overcorrection clarifies the nature of this failure. Overcorrection is defined by magnitude. The system identifies a deviation and applies a response that is too large, causing overshoot and oscillation. Overreaction is defined by timing and frequency. The system applies responses before sufficient evaluation and does so repeatedly in response to short-term variation. Overreaction produces constant instability because the system never settles. Overcorrection produces oscillation because the system repeatedly crosses through alignment. Both are control failures, but they operate through different dimensions of the adjustment process.

Overreaction also interacts with prior mechanisms in specific ways. Measurement provides data that includes both signal and noise. Without evaluation, this data is treated as uniformly actionable. Detection is bypassed in its classification function, allowing noise to be interpreted as deviation. Thresholds lose their role as filters because triggers are activated prematurely or without sufficient confirmation. Monitoring frequency amplifies the problem by increasing exposure to variation without corresponding filtering. Adjustment is applied repeatedly without sufficient basis. The control loop remains intact in structure, but its sequencing is altered. Evaluation is effectively removed, and the loop becomes dominated by reaction.

The temporal progression of the mechanism reflects increasing compression of the control process. In the early stage, reactivity is mild. The system occasionally responds to short-term variation without full evaluation. These responses introduce small inefficiencies but do not prevent stabilization. The system still converges toward alignment because evaluation remains present in most cases. In the mid stage, reaction becomes more frequent. Short-term changes trigger adjustment more consistently. Volatility increases as the system is modified more often than required. Signal clarity declines because adjustments begin to interfere with observation. Stability becomes less consistent, as the system has less time to settle between changes.

In the late stage, reaction dominates the control process. Evaluation is effectively absent. The system responds continuously to observed variation, regardless of its significance. Adjustment cycles occur in rapid succession, and the system does not establish a stable operating state. Each intervention becomes input for the next, creating a self-referential loop of activity. Stability is no longer achievable because the system is never allowed to remain in a fixed configuration long enough to assess alignment.

The failure condition is defined by the replacement of evaluation with reaction. When noise consistently triggers adjustment, and when the system cannot stabilize due to constant change, the control loop becomes functionally destabilizing. The system is governed in form, but not in function. It applies control processes, but those processes degrade alignment rather than preserving it.

The Overreaction Mechanism therefore establishes the requirement for balance within the control system. Responsiveness is necessary to address deviation. However, responsiveness must be constrained by interpretation. Signals must be evaluated before they are acted upon. Variation must be classified before it is corrected. Without this structure, the system confuses movement with misalignment and reacts to conditions that do not require intervention. The result is instability produced by excessive responsiveness.

Stability requires balance between responsiveness and interpretation.

The Misinterpretation Mechanism

The Misinterpretation Mechanism defines the process through which valid data and correctly identified signals are interpreted incorrectly, leading to misclassification of system state and resulting in incorrect adjustment and instability. Measurement may function. Signals may be formed accurately. Detection may identify variation beyond noise. The failure does not occur at the level of data or signal. It occurs at the level of meaning. The system assigns an incorrect interpretation to what it observes, and that interpretation becomes the basis for evaluation and response.

This establishes a critical separation within the control structure. Data does not contain meaning. Signals indicate that variation exists, but they do not specify what that variation represents. Interpretation determines what the system believes is occurring. It converts observation into understanding. When interpretation is correct, evaluation aligns with system reality and adjustment restores alignment. When interpretation is incorrect, evaluation is distorted and adjustment is misapplied. The system acts on a representation of reality that does not correspond to its actual condition.

This mechanism differs from prior control failures in its point of origin. Overreaction reflects premature response. Overcorrection reflects excessive magnitude. Misinterpretation reflects incorrect understanding. The system may respond at the correct time and with an appropriate level of action relative to its interpretation, yet still produce instability because the interpretation itself is wrong. The failure is not in execution. It is in the classification of what the system is responding to.

The distinction between signal and interpretation defines this failure mode. A signal indicates that variation has exceeded a defined noise range. It identifies that something has changed. Interpretation assigns meaning to that change. It determines whether the variation represents a temporary fluctuation, a structural shift, a timing mismatch, or a change in underlying relationships. Without correct interpretation, the signal cannot guide appropriate action. The same signal can lead to different responses depending on how it is understood.

Signal misreading occurs when the system assigns the wrong cause or implication to a valid signal. The signal itself is not in error. It correctly indicates that variation exists. The misinterpretation arises in determining what that variation means for system alignment. A decline in liquidity may be interpreted as structural weakness, implying that the system's buffer is insufficient relative to its obligations. It may also represent a temporary timing shift, where inflow and outflow are misaligned in sequence but not in structure. The signal is identical. The implications are not. If interpreted as structural weakness, the system may attempt to increase liquidity buffers or reduce obligations. If interpreted as a timing shift, the system may adjust sequencing without altering structural relationships. Misinterpretation leads to selecting the wrong response for the actual condition.

The same dynamic applies across system components. An increase in expenses may indicate a baseline shift in load, requiring structural adjustment to maintain capacity alignment. It may also represent a transient fluctuation that resolves without altering long-term relationships. Income variability may reflect a change in reliability, requiring recalibration of expectations, or a short-term deviation within an otherwise stable pattern. Exposure changes may indicate increased concentration risk or temporary movement within acceptable bounds.

In each case, the signal identifies variation. Interpretation determines its meaning. Incorrect interpretation produces a response that does not correspond to the system's actual state.

This error is amplified when data is interpreted without context. Data represents isolated values or changes. Context defines the relationships within which those values exist. Without context, data cannot be meaningfully evaluated. A reduction in income magnitude may appear significant in isolation. Without reference to timing, duration, or prior variability, it cannot be classified as structural or temporary. An increase in expense level may appear destabilizing when viewed alone. Without comparison to capacity, liquidity, and historical baseline, its impact on alignment cannot be determined.

Context consists of relational and temporal positioning. Relational context defines how components interact. Income must be evaluated relative to expense load. Liquidity must be evaluated relative to obligations and timing. Exposure must be evaluated relative to concentration and sensitivity. Temporal context defines how variation evolves over time. A single data point does not establish persistence. It does not indicate whether a change is part of a trend or a deviation within a stable range. Interpretation requires both forms of context. Without them, signals are assigned meaning based on incomplete information.

Data without context produces ambiguity. The system must still interpret the signal, but the interpretation is not anchored to sufficient information. This increases the probability of misclassification. The same data point may be interpreted as indicating stability or instability depending on assumed context. If those assumptions are incorrect, the resulting interpretation is incorrect. The system therefore acts on a representation of its state that does not reflect actual relationships.

Misinterpretation produces two primary error types: false positives and missed signals. A false positive occurs when the system identifies meaningful deviation where none exists. A signal is overinterpreted, and normal variation is classified as structural misalignment. This leads to unnecessary adjustment. The system modifies its configuration in response to a condition that does not require intervention. This introduces instability by altering relationships that were previously within stable bounds.

A missed signal occurs when the system fails to recognize meaningful deviation. Variation that represents a change in alignment is interpreted as noise or temporary fluctuation. This leads to delayed or absent adjustment. The system continues to operate without correcting deviation that requires intervention. This allows misalignment to accumulate, reducing margin and increasing sensitivity. Both error types originate from incorrect interpretation. The data is present. The signal is formed. The failure occurs in assigning meaning.

These errors are symmetrical in effect. False positives introduce instability through unnecessary change. Missed signals introduce instability through lack of required change. In both cases, the system's response does not correspond to its actual condition. The control loop remains active, but it operates on incorrect understanding. Adjustment is applied, but not to the correct problem. Stability is therefore not restored.

Decision distortion is the direct consequence of misinterpretation. Decisions within the system are based on evaluated meaning. When interpretation is incorrect, evaluation is incorrect. Decisions therefore reflect a distorted representation of system state. Adjustment is applied to the wrong domain, at the wrong time, or with the wrong magnitude relative to actual conditions. The system may attempt to correct liquidity when the issue is structural expense load. It may adjust expense structure when the issue is temporary income timing. It may alter exposure when the underlying problem is capacity imbalance.

This distortion operates along multiple dimensions. Directional distortion occurs when the system applies the wrong type of adjustment. Timing distortion occurs when the system responds too early or too late relative to the actual persistence of variation. Magnitude distortion occurs when the system applies a scale of adjustment that corresponds to the interpreted condition rather than the actual one. In each case, the adjustment may be internally consistent with the interpretation. It is misaligned with the system's true state because the interpretation is incorrect.

The system-level consequences of misinterpretation are cumulative. Adjustments do not resolve misalignment because they are not targeted at its actual source. The system experiences repeated ineffective adjustments. Each intervention changes system configuration, but does not restore alignment. This can lead to persistent instability, as the system continually modifies itself without converging toward a stable state. Signal reliability declines because the relationship between observed variation and resulting system behavior becomes inconsistent. The system appears responsive and actively controlled, yet its actions do not align with underlying conditions.

This condition is structurally distinct from other failure modes. In neglect, the system fails because control processes are absent. In overreaction, the system fails because response occurs too quickly and too frequently. In overcorrection, the system fails because response magnitude is excessive. In misinterpretation, the system fails because response is based on incorrect meaning. The control loop is active. Measurement is functioning. Detection is occurring. Adjustment is being applied. The failure arises because the system does not correctly understand what it is observing.

The mechanism interacts directly with prior components of the control system. Measurement provides data that reflects system activity. Signal formation identifies variation beyond noise. Detection flags potential deviation. Interpretation assigns meaning to that deviation. If interpretation is incorrect, all subsequent processes are affected. Threshold evaluation is applied to a misclassified condition. Triggers may be activated or suppressed incorrectly. Adjustment is selected based on incorrect evaluation. The entire control process is therefore corrupted at the interpretive layer.

This dependency establishes interpretation as a central function of governance. Measurement and detection are necessary but not sufficient for stability. They provide visibility, but not understanding. Interpretation converts visibility into actionable meaning. Without correct interpretation, the system cannot distinguish between types of variation or determine appropriate response. Control processes remain active, but they operate on incorrect inputs. Stability cannot be achieved under these conditions because alignment requires correspondence between system state and system response.

The temporal progression of misinterpretation reflects increasing distortion of system understanding. In the early stage, misinterpretation occurs occasionally. Most signals are correctly understood, and adjustment generally restores alignment. The system remains stable because errors are limited in frequency and impact. In the mid stage, misclassification becomes more frequent. Signals are interpreted inconsistently, leading to a mix of correct and incorrect adjustments. Stability becomes less consistent because the system's responses do not reliably correspond to its state.

In the late stage, interpretation is consistently incorrect. The system's understanding of its own condition is fundamentally misaligned with reality. Control processes operate continuously, but they produce instability because they are based on incorrect meaning. Adjustment cannot restore alignment because it is not directed at the actual sources of misalignment. The system cannot converge because its reference for evaluation is incorrect.

Failure occurs when interpretation consistently misrepresents system state, evaluation is based on incorrect meaning, and adjustment no longer corresponds to actual conditions. At this point, the system is actively controlled, but persistently misaligned. The presence of control does not produce stability because the content of control is incorrect. The system's actions are coherent relative to its interpretation, but incoherent relative to reality.

The Misinterpretation Mechanism therefore establishes the final dependency within the control framework. Stability requires accurate measurement, correct detection, appropriate threshold definition, and effective adjustment. Each of these processes depends on interpretation. Interpretation determines how data is understood, how signals are classified, and how deviation is evaluated. When interpretation is incorrect, the entire control process is misaligned, regardless of how well other components function.

Interpretation determines outcome.

The Complexity Creep Mechanism

The Complexity Creep Mechanism defines the process through which repeated adjustments, layered corrections, and accumulated structural changes increase system complexity, reduce clarity and transparency, and diminish the controllability of the financial system over time. The system does not become complex by design in a single step. It becomes complex through the accumulation of prior control actions. Each intervention modifies structure. Each modification persists. Over time, these modifications interact, producing a system that is more difficult to interpret and more difficult to control than its original configuration.

This mechanism differs from prior failure modes in its origin. Neglect produces instability through absence of control. Overreaction and overcorrection produce instability through misapplied control. Misinterpretation produces instability through incorrect understanding. Complexity creep produces instability even when control processes are functioning and interpretation is not fundamentally incorrect. The degradation arises because the system itself becomes harder to govern. Control does not disappear. It becomes less effective relative to the structure it must operate on.

The system begins in a relatively simple state. Relationships between income, expenses, liquidity, and exposure are direct and observable. Control pathways are clear. Measurement produces data that can be interpreted with minimal ambiguity. Detection identifies deviation that can be traced to identifiable causes. Adjustment produces outcomes that can be anticipated with reasonable accuracy. In this state, the control loop operates with high clarity. Cause and effect are visible. Interventions have predictable impact.

Over time, adjustments accumulate. Each correction is applied to address a specific deviation. A change in expense structure may be introduced to manage load. A liquidity buffer may be reallocated to address timing mismatch. Exposure may be redistributed to reduce sensitivity. Each of these actions solves a localized problem. Each also modifies the system's structure. These modifications are not temporary. They persist as part of the system's configuration. The system therefore begins to incorporate its own history of correction.

This accumulation produces layering. The system no longer reflects only its original design. It reflects the sequence of adjustments that have been applied to maintain alignment over time. Each layer represents a prior solution. These layers do not replace one another. They coexist. The system contains legacy structures that were introduced under different conditions. It contains constraints that were designed to address past deviations. It contains relationships that have been modified incrementally rather than holistically. The result is a system composed of multiple overlapping configurations.

Complexity accumulation is persistent. Structural layers introduced through prior adjustments are not automatically removed when the conditions that produced them no longer exist. A constraint introduced to address a specific deviation may remain in place even after that deviation has resolved. A buffer configuration designed for a prior condition may persist even when system requirements have changed. The system therefore retains historical structure regardless of current necessity. Complexity does not recede as conditions normalize. It remains embedded in the system, shaping future behavior even when its original purpose is no longer active.

This layered structure reduces clarity. Clarity is defined as the ability to understand system relationships and trace cause-effect pathways. In a simple system, a change in one component produces an observable effect in another. The pathway between cause and effect is direct. As complexity increases, these pathways become indirect. A change in income may affect liquidity through multiple intermediate relationships. An adjustment in expense structure may interact with prior constraints in ways that are not immediately visible. Exposure changes may propagate through multiple dependencies before producing observable impact.

As these pathways multiply, interpretation becomes more difficult. The same signal no longer corresponds to a single identifiable cause. It may be the result of multiple interacting factors. A liquidity decline may reflect expense structure, income variability, prior buffer adjustments, or interactions between them. Without clear pathways, the system cannot easily determine which component is responsible for observed variation. This ambiguity reduces the reliability of interpretation. Signals become harder to classify because their origins are obscured.

Reduced clarity affects detection and evaluation. Detection identifies that variation has occurred. Evaluation requires understanding what that variation represents. When relationships are complex, evaluation becomes less certain. The system may identify a deviation but cannot easily determine whether it is structural or temporary, isolated or systemic, or driven by one component or multiple interacting components. This uncertainty introduces variability into the control process. The same signal may be interpreted differently under similar conditions because the underlying relationships are not transparent.

Controllability declines as a result. Controllability is defined as the ability to predict the outcome of an adjustment and apply targeted correction. In a simple system, adjustments produce relatively direct effects. A change in one component leads to a corresponding change in system position. As complexity increases, adjustments interact with multiple components simultaneously. Each intervention has more points of contact within the system. The effect of an adjustment is therefore distributed across multiple pathways.

This distribution introduces unintended consequences. An adjustment intended to correct one relationship may alter others. A change in liquidity allocation may affect exposure sensitivity. A modification of expense structure may interact with prior constraints, producing effects that were not anticipated. Because these interactions are not fully visible, the outcome of adjustment becomes less predictable. Control loses precision. The system can still be adjusted, but the effect of adjustment cannot be isolated as easily.

This persistence creates asymmetry between accumulation and reduction. Complexity increases through each adjustment, but it is not reduced through ordinary operation. The control loop is designed to correct deviation, not to remove structural layers that were introduced by prior correction. As a result, the system evolves in one direction with respect to complexity. It becomes more structured over time, but not necessarily more controllable. This asymmetry contributes to the gradual degradation of governance effectiveness even when control processes continue to function.

This produces a fundamental tradeoff between structure and control. Additional structure increases the number of control options available. The system can be modified in more ways. However, each additional layer reduces transparency. The system becomes more difficult to interpret and more difficult to predict. In a simple system, fewer control options exist, but their effects are clear. In a complex system, more control options exist, but their effects are less certain. Beyond a certain point, the increase in available control pathways is offset by the reduction in clarity and predictability. Effective control declines even though structural capability has increased.

Interaction effects amplify this tradeoff. As components become more interconnected, each adjustment propagates through multiple pathways. The system exhibits indirect dependencies. A change applied in one domain affects others through relationships that may not be immediately visible. These interactions are not linear. They may reinforce or offset each other depending on configuration. This makes it difficult to isolate cause and effect. The system's response to intervention becomes context-dependent. The same adjustment may produce different outcomes depending on the state of other components.

This complexity degrades feedback quality. Measurement continues to produce data. Signals continue to identify variation. However, the interpretation of those signals becomes less reliable because the system's structure obscures the relationship between observation and cause. Detection may identify deviation, but evaluation cannot confidently classify it. Feedback no longer provides clear guidance for adjustment. It reflects a system whose internal relationships are difficult to resolve into discrete causes.

As feedback degrades, the system may compensate by increasing control activity. More frequent observation, more detailed measurement, and more frequent adjustment may be applied in an attempt to restore clarity. However, these responses add further structure to the system. The attempt to improve control introduces additional complexity, which further obscures relationships and reduces interpretability. This creates a reinforcing cycle in which complexity generates degraded feedback, and degraded feedback leads to additional structure, increasing complexity further.

As feedback degrades, the control loop loses effectiveness. The loop still operates in form. Observation occurs. Signals are generated. Adjustments are applied. However, each stage operates with reduced precision. Measurement captures data that is more difficult to interpret. Detection identifies variation that cannot be easily classified. Adjustment is applied to conditions that are not fully understood. The loop does not fail. It becomes less reliable in producing alignment.

System-level consequences emerge from this degradation. Response becomes slower because uncertainty increases the time required to interpret signals. Incorrect response becomes more likely because interpretation is less certain. Overcorrection may occur because the system compensates for uncertainty by applying larger adjustments. Underreaction may occur because ambiguity reduces confidence in intervention. These outcomes are not the result of specific control errors. They are the result of operating within a system whose complexity exceeds the capacity of the control processes to manage it effectively.

The system therefore exhibits a distinct condition. It remains actively governed. Control processes are present and functioning. However, the effectiveness of those processes declines. Adjustments do not consistently restore alignment. Signals do not consistently produce correct evaluation. The system's behavior becomes less predictable. Stability becomes more difficult to maintain, not because control is absent, but because the system has become too complex to control with the same level of precision.

The temporal progression of complexity creep reflects this accumulation. In the early stage, the system remains relatively simple. Adjustments are applied, but their number is limited. Relationships remain clear. Control processes operate effectively because the system's structure is still transparent. In the mid stage, layering becomes noticeable. Multiple adjustments have been incorporated into the system. Interaction effects increase. Relationships become less direct. Control processes remain functional, but require greater effort to interpret signals and predict outcomes.

In the late stage, complexity becomes dominant. The system contains a significant number of accumulated structures. Relationships between components are difficult to trace. Feedback is degraded. Control processes operate with reduced effectiveness because they cannot fully interpret or predict system behavior. The system is governed in form, but not in function. It continues to be monitored and adjusted, but those processes no longer produce consistent alignment.

Failure occurs when system complexity exceeds the ability to interpret and control it. At this point, the control loop cannot accurately evaluate system state or reliably apply effective adjustment. The system does not become ungoverned. It becomes ungovernable within its existing structure because the accumulated complexity exceeds the capacity of the control loop to interpret system state and apply targeted correction with sufficient precision. The processes of control remain active, but they no longer produce stability because the system's complexity has outpaced the capacity of those processes to manage it.

This mechanism completes the structural evolution of governance failure. The system begins with clear relationships and effective control. Through repeated adjustment, it accumulates structure. That structure reduces clarity and predictability. Control processes become less effective, even as they remain active. Instability emerges not from absence of control, nor from misapplication alone, but from the increasing difficulty of governing a system whose structure has become layered and interconnected.

Simplicity improves governance.

The Alignment Maintenance Mechanism

Stability is commonly interpreted as a condition that can be reached. A system is configured, relationships are balanced, and once the correct structure is in place, stability is assumed to persist. This interpretation treats stability as an outcome of prior decisions, something established and then retained. This framing does not hold under continuous operation. A financial system does not pause after configuration. Its components continue to change. Income fluctuates in magnitude and timing. Expenses shift in both structure and variability. Liquidity is consumed, replenished, and reallocated. Exposure evolves as dependencies and sensitivities change. These movements are not periodic. They are continuous. A system that is continuously moving cannot remain stable through static configuration. Stability cannot be a fixed state because the system itself does not remain fixed. The Alignment Maintenance Mechanism defines the process through which stability is preserved under these conditions. It is the continuous repositioning of the system within a bounded range of acceptable relationships as those relationships evolve over time. Stability is not achieved and then maintained passively. It is maintained actively through continuous positioning. A system is stable not because it has reached the correct configuration, but because it remains within acceptable bounds as it changes.

Stability must first be separated from the idea of a precise point. If stability were defined as a single configuration, then any deviation from that configuration would represent instability. Under this model, variation itself becomes a failure condition. This would imply that a stable system must eliminate movement to remain stable. This does not reflect the behavior of financial systems. Income does not remain constant. Expenses do not remain fixed. Liquidity is not static. Exposure is not unchanging. Variation exists even in systems that are structurally stable. Therefore, stability cannot be defined as the absence of movement or adherence to a single configuration. Stability exists as a range. This range represents the set of conditions under which system relationships remain aligned. Within this range, variation occurs without compromising structural integrity. Outside this range, variation alters system relationships in ways that produce instability. The range is defined through the interaction of core system variables. Income must remain sufficient relative to expenses to support ongoing load. Liquidity must remain sufficient relative to obligations to provide time under variability. Exposure must remain within tolerance to prevent disproportionate impact under adverse conditions. These relationships do not exist at exact values. They exist within boundaries. As long as the system operates within those boundaries, it remains stable. The implication is structural. A system does not need to maintain exact conditions to remain stable. It needs to remain within acceptable limits. Movement within those limits is not failure. It is the expected behavior of a functioning system.

Because the system is always moving within this range, stability depends on continuous positioning rather than periodic correction. Position represents the current configuration of relationships between system components. Alignment represents whether that position falls within the defined stability range. These definitions establish that alignment is not static. It is not a condition that persists automatically once achieved. It must be continuously maintained because the underlying relationships are continuously changing. Income timing shifts alter short-term capacity. Expense variability changes load distribution. Liquidity levels rise and fall as buffers are used and replenished. Exposure shifts as dependencies evolve. Each of these movements changes system position. If positioning is not continuously maintained, these movements accumulate. Accumulated movement eventually pushes the system outside its stability range. The system does not remain aligned on its own. It is kept aligned through ongoing repositioning. This repositioning does not require constant large adjustments. It requires continuous small alignment actions that keep the system within bounds as it evolves.

This leads to a necessary distinction between variability and instability. Variability is normal system movement within the stability range. It is continuous and expected. It reflects the natural fluctuation of income, expenses, liquidity, and exposure. Variability does not alter system relationships in a way that threatens stability. It remains contained within acceptable limits. Instability is movement beyond those limits. It represents a change in relationships that the system cannot absorb without corrective action. Instability requires adjustment because the system has moved outside its stable operating range. The distinction is structural, not observational. All systems are variable. Not all systems are unstable. Misclassifying variability as instability introduces unnecessary adjustment. Misclassifying instability as variability allows misalignment to persist. Both errors disrupt alignment maintenance. Accurate classification ensures that movement within bounds is allowed to occur without intervention, while movement beyond bounds is addressed appropriately. Stability depends on this separation because it prevents unnecessary disruption while ensuring necessary correction. Variability is absorbed within the system's existing structure. Instability is transmitted through it, altering relationships and requiring intervention.

Stability therefore cannot be understood as the absence of movement. It must be understood as the containment of movement. Movement is constant. The system is always changing. Stability exists only when that movement is contained within defined limits. The role of control is not to eliminate variation but to ensure that variation remains bounded. Measurement captures movement as it occurs. Detection classifies that movement as variation or deviation. Thresholds define the boundaries of acceptable movement. Adjustment repositions the system when those boundaries are approached or crossed. The Alignment Maintenance Mechanism integrates these functions into a continuous process. It ensures that movement does not accumulate into deviation by maintaining system position within acceptable bounds at all times. Without this containment, even small variations can accumulate into instability. With containment, even continuous variation does not compromise stability.

This distinction also clarifies the difference between maintenance and correction. Correction occurs after deviation. The system moves outside its stability range, and adjustment is required to restore alignment. Maintenance occurs before deviation becomes significant. It operates continuously to prevent the system from leaving its stability range in the first place. Correction is reactive to deviation. Maintenance is continuous containment of system movement before deviation emerges. Systems that rely primarily on correction allow deviation to develop before responding. Systems that maintain alignment continuously reduce the need for correction by preventing deviation from accumulating. The absence of maintenance increases reliance on correction. This produces cycles of drift followed by intervention. Continuous maintenance reduces these cycles by keeping the system within bounds as it evolves.

The time dimension of alignment reinforces this structure. Alignment is not evaluated at discrete moments and then assumed to persist. It must be continuously re-established because system position changes continuously. At each moment, the relationship between income, expenses, liquidity, and exposure is slightly different. These changes may be small, but they are persistent. Without continuous positioning, these small changes accumulate. That accumulation is not linear. Each small change alters the context in which subsequent changes occur. Reduced liquidity increases sensitivity to income variability. Increased expense rigidity amplifies the effect of timing shifts. These interactions cause positioning errors to compound rather than remain isolated. Without continuous maintenance, the system does not drift evenly. It accelerates toward misalignment as small deviations interact over time. Accumulation eventually produces deviation. Stability exists only as long as the system is actively maintained within its stability range.

The source of system movement must also be made explicit. Income variability introduces changes in capacity. Expense fluctuation alters load. Liquidity changes affect available time and buffer. Exposure shifts modify system sensitivity. These movements occur independently and interact with one another. Maintenance ensures that these interactions do not produce compounding effects that push the system outside its bounds. By continuously repositioning the system, maintenance prevents small changes from interacting in ways that create larger deviations. This prevents accumulation, reduces compounding effects, and preserves alignment over time.

This continuous positioning can be understood as operating within a stability envelope. The envelope defines the boundaries of acceptable system positioning. Within this envelope, movement is allowed and expected. Outside this envelope, movement produces instability. The system is not static within the envelope. It moves continuously. Maintenance ensures that this movement remains contained. Exiting the envelope represents failure of containment. Remaining within the envelope represents successful alignment maintenance. The envelope does not eliminate movement. It defines the space within which movement can occur without compromising stability.

Failure of the Alignment Maintenance Mechanism occurs when continuous positioning is not maintained. The system continues to move, but repositioning does not occur with sufficient consistency. Movement accumulates within the stability range. Over time, this accumulation pushes the system toward the boundary of the envelope. Without continuous positioning, the system crosses that boundary. Instability emerges not from a single large deviation but from accumulated small movements that were not contained. Failure also occurs when variability is misinterpreted or ignored. Misinterpretation leads to inappropriate positioning, either through unnecessary adjustment or lack of required adjustment. In both cases, alignment becomes inconsistent. The system alternates between periods of stability and instability because positioning is not continuously maintained.

The progression of this mechanism follows a clear pattern. In the early stage, movement remains within bounds and positioning is continuous. Variability is absorbed without producing instability. The system remains aligned because movement is contained. In the mid stage, positioning becomes inconsistent. The system still operates within bounds, but small deviations begin to accumulate. Alignment is maintained intermittently rather than continuously. This increases the likelihood of boundary breach. In the late stage, containment is lost. The system exits the stability range more frequently. Correction replaces maintenance as the dominant process. Stability becomes reactive rather than continuous. The system no longer maintains alignment as it moves. It attempts to restore alignment after deviation has already occurred.

The boundary condition of this mechanism defines its failure state. Failure occurs when stability is treated as a fixed condition rather than a continuously maintained position. If alignment is assumed to persist without ongoing positioning, the system will drift. Alternatively, failure occurs when the system relies on periodic correction rather than continuous maintenance. In this condition, alignment degrades between interventions. The system repeatedly exits its stability range and requires restoration. In both cases, the absence of continuous positioning allows misalignment to develop.

The implication is direct. Stability cannot be achieved and left in place. It must be maintained because the system is continuously changing. Alignment is not a state. It is a process. It exists only as long as the system is actively positioned within its stability bounds. Stability is maintained positioning because financial systems do not remain aligned on their own. They must be continuously positioned within stable bounds as conditions change.

The Regime Change Mechanism

The Regime Change Mechanism defines how financial systems respond when underlying conditions shift in a way that invalidates prior assumptions, requiring structural adaptation rather than incremental adjustment. A system operates within an environment that is not fixed. Conditions that shape income behavior, expense stability, liquidity requirements, and exposure sensitivity can change in ways that are not temporary deviations but structural transitions. When this occurs, the system is no longer operating under the same rules that previously governed its stability. The mechanism is not concerned with variation within a stable environment. It addresses the condition in which the environment itself changes, and with it, the validity of the system's internal model.

The first requirement is to distinguish between temporary shifts and structural shifts. Temporary shifts represent variation within an existing framework. The system's assumptions remain valid, even if conditions temporarily move outside typical ranges. Income may fluctuate, expenses may rise or fall, liquidity may compress or expand, and exposure may shift. These changes occur within a structure that still holds. The system can absorb them, or it can correct for them using established mechanisms. Adjustment and maintenance are sufficient because the relationships between components remain consistent. Structural shifts are different. They alter the underlying relationships that define system behavior. What was previously stable may no longer be stable under the same configuration. What was previously predictable may become variable. What was previously contained may become amplified. The system is no longer operating within the same structure, even if the observed signals appear similar.

The distinction is not based on the size of the change alone. It is defined by persistence and by the effect on system relationships. A temporary shift may be large but short-lived, allowing the system to return to its prior configuration. A structural shift may begin with small changes that persist and alter how components interact over time. The same observed signal can belong to either category. A decline in income may represent a temporary disruption within a stable pattern, or it may represent a shift in income reliability that changes the system's capacity structure. An increase in expenses may be transient, or it may reflect a permanent increase in baseline load. The classification determines the required response. Temporary shifts require absorption or correction. Structural shifts require adaptation because the model used to interpret and respond to those signals is no longer valid.

Not all change requires adaptation. Only structural change invalidates the model itself.

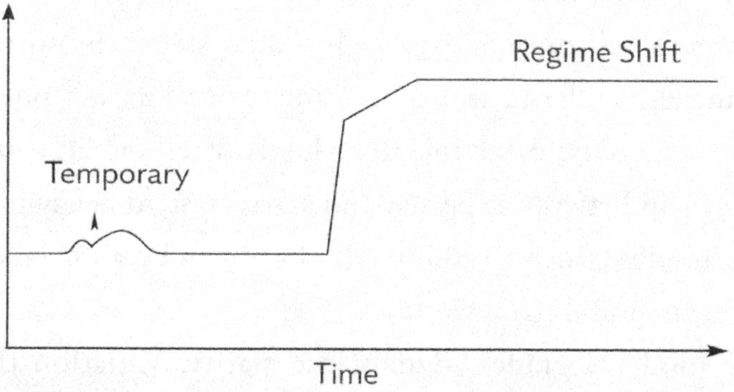

[Figure 8: Regime Shift vs Temporary Deviation]

A financial system does not operate without a model, whether explicit or implicit. The model defines expectations about how the system behaves. It includes assumptions about income continuity, expense variability, liquidity sufficiency, and exposure impact. These assumptions shape how signals are interpreted, how thresholds are defined, and how adjustments are applied. When conditions remain consistent, the model provides a reliable framework for maintaining alignment. When conditions change structurally, the model begins to fail. This failure does not occur immediately as a visible breakdown. It emerges through inconsistencies between expected and actual behavior. Signals that were previously predictable become erratic. Adjustments that previously restored alignment lose effectiveness. The system responds, but the responses do not produce convergence. Instead, they produce repeated cycles of misalignment.

Model breakdown is not the absence of response. It is the persistence of response under incorrect assumptions. The system continues to apply adjustment based on relationships that no longer hold. Income variability may increase, but the system continues to treat income as stable. Expense rigidity may rise, but the system continues to treat expenses as flexible. Liquidity requirements may expand, but the system continues to operate with insufficient buffers. Exposure sensitivity may increase, but the system continues to assume prior tolerance levels. Each of these mismatches produces a gap between expected and actual system behavior. This gap cannot be resolved through additional adjustment because the adjustment is based on an invalid framework.

As the model degrades, signals lose clarity. Variation that would previously be classified accurately becomes difficult to interpret. The system may identify deviation, but it cannot correctly determine its nature. Temporary variation may be mistaken for structural change, or structural change may be treated as temporary. Adjustment cycles increase in frequency or scale without restoring alignment. The system appears active, but the activity does not produce stability. This condition reflects a fundamental limitation. A system cannot stabilize if the model it uses to interpret and respond to conditions no longer reflects reality.

The response to model breakdown is not increased adjustment. It is the updating of system configuration. Adaptation requires redefining the assumptions that govern system behavior. This includes re-evaluating income reliability, expense structure, liquidity requirements, and exposure tolerance. These elements must be realigned with current conditions rather than prior expectations. This process is structurally distinct from both adjustment and recalibration. Adjustment modifies system position within an existing framework. Recalibration resets the baseline within that framework. Regime change requires redefining the framework itself.

When income behavior changes structurally, the system must treat income differently. Variability that was previously minimal may become persistent. This changes how capacity is defined and how much reliance can be placed on expected inflow. When expenses become more rigid, the system's load structure changes. Flexibility is reduced, and the system becomes more sensitive to variation in capacity. When liquidity requirements expand, the buffers that were previously sufficient are no longer adequate to maintain stability. The system must redefine the level and accessibility of liquidity required to sustain operations. When exposure sensitivity increases, the tolerance for variation decreases. Dependencies that were previously manageable may become sources of instability.

These changes do not occur in isolation. They interact. A shift in income reliability affects liquidity requirements. Increased expense rigidity affects tolerance for income variability. Changes in exposure sensitivity affect how much deviation can be absorbed without destabilization. Updating system configuration requires redefining these relationships as a set, not as isolated components. The system must be restructured to reflect the new conditions under which it operates.

The primary failure mode within this mechanism is persistence risk. Systems are structured to assume continuity. They are designed based on observed patterns and relationships that are expected to hold over time. When those patterns change, the system does not immediately recognize the shift. It continues to operate under the assumption that the prior model remains valid. This produces a lag between environmental change and system adaptation. During this lag, the system continues to apply adjustment to restore alignment within a framework that no longer applies.

Persistence risk is not the absence of response. It is the continuation of response under outdated assumptions. The system detects deviation and attempts to correct it. However, because the underlying relationships have changed, these corrections do not restore alignment. Instead, they produce repeated cycles of misalignment. The system may oscillate between states or drift further from stability. Each failed correction increases the gap between the system's configuration and the conditions it faces. Over time, this gap becomes too large to be managed through incremental adjustment.

The consequences of persistence risk are cumulative. Repeated failed corrections consume resources and reduce system flexibility. Misalignment increases as the system attempts to force alignment within an outdated structure. Oscillation may emerge as the system alternates between over-adjustment and under-adjustment. Drift may continue as the system fails to recognize the need for structural change. Eventually, the system reaches a point where the existing configuration cannot support stability under current conditions. At this point, breakdown occurs not because the system failed to act, but because it acted within an invalid model.

Persistence is not stability. It is delayed recognition of change.

The transition required by the Regime Change Mechanism is from continuity to adaptation. Stability depends on the system's ability to align with current conditions, not past conditions. This requires recognizing when the environment has changed in a way that invalidates prior assumptions. It also requires redefining system behavior to match those conditions. Systems that fail to adapt continue to optimize an outdated structure. Systems that remain stable evolve their structure to maintain alignment with the environment in which they operate.

This evolution is not continuous in the same way as alignment maintenance. It occurs when structural shifts accumulate to a point where the existing model no longer applies. At that point, the system must transition to a new configuration that reflects the new regime. This transition may involve changes in how capacity is defined, how load is structured, how liquidity is managed, and how exposure is distributed. The objective is not to restore prior stability, but to establish stability under new conditions.

The mechanism operates within the broader system of governance. Measurement captures changes in system behavior. Detection identifies deviation. Thresholds define limits. Adjustment attempts to restore alignment. Recalibration resets baselines when those baselines no longer reflect current conditions. The Regime Change Mechanism sits above these processes. It determines when the entire framework within which these processes operate must be updated. Without this mechanism, the system continues to operate with tools that are no longer suited to the environment it faces.

The failure to recognize regime change produces a specific pattern. Signals become inconsistent. Adjustment cycles increase in frequency or magnitude. Alignment is not restored despite continued intervention. The system appears active, but the activity does not produce stability. This pattern reflects the persistence of an outdated model. Recognition of this pattern is necessary to trigger adaptation. Without it, the system continues to degrade as it attempts to correct within an invalid structure.

The implication is structural and non-negotiable. Stability cannot be maintained by preserving prior assumptions when conditions have changed. It requires updating those assumptions to reflect the current environment. Systems that do not evolve remain aligned to conditions that no longer exist. Systems that evolve maintain alignment by redefining their structure to match current conditions.

Systems must evolve because stability depends on alignment with current conditions, not past assumptions.

The Governance Under Stress Mechanism

The Governance Under Stress Mechanism defines how a financial system operates when conditions compress capacity, reduce margin, and force the control process to function under constraint, revealing the true structure of the system. A system that appears stable under normal conditions is not fully observed. Stability in unconstrained conditions does not require the system to engage its full structure. It does not require buffers to be consumed, nor does it require control processes to operate at their limits. Under these conditions, weaknesses remain latent because they are not tested. Stress changes this condition. It introduces constraint. It reduces the distance between current system position and failure boundaries. It forces the system to operate with limited margin, exposing how it actually behaves when variation cannot be absorbed passively.

Stress is not an anomaly. It is a condition in which the system is required to operate with reduced capacity relative to load, increased variability, or compressed buffers. These conditions are not external to the system. They are part of its operating environment. Stress emerges when the relationship between capacity and demand shifts in a way that reduces tolerance for variation. This may occur through reduced income stability, increased expense rigidity, diminished liquidity, or increased exposure sensitivity. Each of these shifts narrows the system's stability range. Movement that would previously remain within bounds now approaches or exceeds those bounds more quickly. The system is not necessarily experiencing a new type of variation. It is experiencing variation within a tighter structure.

Under stable conditions, system behavior appears smooth. Variation is absorbed without requiring continuous intervention. Minor deviations do not produce visible instability. This creates the appearance of robustness. However, this appearance is incomplete. The system has not been required to demonstrate how it behaves when its buffers are engaged or when its control processes are constrained. Stress introduces this requirement. It removes the excess capacity that allows variation to be absorbed without consequence. As a result, the system's structure becomes visible.

Systems do not reveal their structure under normal conditions. They reveal it under stress.

Under stress, latent dependencies become explicit. Relationships that were previously buffered become direct. A dependency on a single income source may not be visible when income is stable, but becomes critical when that income fluctuates. Expense rigidity may not create pressure when capacity is high, but becomes restrictive when capacity tightens. Liquidity sufficiency may appear adequate until it is actively consumed. Exposure concentration may remain hidden until variation produces disproportionate impact. These conditions do not emerge because stress introduces new structure. They emerge because stress removes the margin that was previously masking existing structure.

The first observable effect of stress is buffer utilization. Buffers represent the system's ability to absorb variation without immediate adjustment. They include liquidity reserves, flexible expense structures, redundant capacity sources, and margin between income and load. Under stable conditions, buffers are present but not fully engaged. They exist as latent capacity. Under stress, buffers are not only present; they are used. The system begins to draw on liquidity to sustain operations when income becomes uncertain. Expense flexibility is used to adjust load when capacity tightens. Redundancy is activated when primary sources become unreliable. Margin is consumed as variation exceeds normal ranges.

This progression follows a clear structure. In the early stage of stress, buffers absorb variation with minimal disruption. The system continues to operate within its stability range, but with reduced margin. Control processes remain effective because there is still sufficient capacity to respond. In the mid stage, buffers compress. The system continues to operate, but the available margin decreases. The ability to absorb additional variation without adjustment is reduced. Control processes must operate more precisely because errors consume a larger proportion of remaining capacity. In the late stage, buffers deplete. The system approaches the boundary of its stability range. Variation that would previously be absorbed now produces immediate pressure. The system's ability to sustain operations without structural change becomes limited.

Buffers determine how long a system can operate under constraint before instability emerges. The depth of buffers defines the time available for the system to respond to stress. Deeper buffers allow the system to sustain operations while adjusting to changing conditions. Shallow buffers compress this time, forcing more immediate response. The structure of buffers determines what types of stress can be absorbed. Liquidity buffers absorb timing mismatches between inflow and outflow. Expense flexibility absorbs changes in capacity. Redundancy absorbs disruptions in specific components. Margin absorbs general variability. A system's ability to operate under stress is therefore not determined solely by the presence of buffers, but by how those buffers are structured relative to the types of variation encountered.

As buffers are consumed, the control process itself changes. Governance does not disappear under stress. It becomes constrained. The control loop—observation, evaluation, adjustment—continues to operate, but under different conditions. The quality of input degrades because signals become more volatile and less distinguishable from noise. Measurement continues, but interpretation becomes more difficult as variation increases. Detection remains active, but classification becomes more uncertain as conditions change rapidly. Thresholds remain in place, but the distance to those thresholds decreases, reducing tolerance for error. Adjustment remains possible, but the scale and timing of adjustments become more sensitive.

Control under stress is not removed. It is restricted.

This restriction operates across multiple dimensions. First, the number of available options decreases. Under stable conditions, the system can choose between multiple adjustment pathways with limited consequence. Under stress, these options narrow. Certain adjustments may no longer be viable because they require capacity that is no longer available. Second, tradeoffs become more rigid. Adjustments that affect one component have more immediate and significant effects on others because buffers that would normally absorb these interactions are reduced. Third, the cost of error increases. Under stable conditions, incorrect adjustment may produce limited disruption. Under stress, the same error consumes a larger proportion of remaining capacity, accelerating movement toward instability.

Timing also compresses under stress. The interval between detection and required response shortens because the system has less capacity to absorb ongoing variation. Delayed response that would previously be acceptable now results in boundary breach. This compression reduces the system's ability to operate with extended evaluation cycles. Decisions must be made with less time and less margin for correction. This does not eliminate the need for evaluation. It increases the consequences of incomplete evaluation.

Adjustment under these conditions remains necessary, but its characteristics change. The scale of acceptable adjustment narrows because large changes can produce unintended consequences that cannot be absorbed. Incremental adjustments become more sensitive because each change interacts with a system that has reduced buffering capacity. Coordination across system components becomes more critical because changes in one area propagate more directly to others. The control process must operate within these constraints, maintaining alignment with fewer degrees of freedom.

Failure points emerge when these constraints exceed the system's structural capacity. Failure is not a discrete event that occurs independently of prior conditions. It is the result of progressive constraint. As buffers are consumed and control becomes restricted, the system approaches points at which it can no longer maintain alignment. These points represent breakdowns in specific system relationships.

Liquidity failure occurs when the system cannot meet obligations in time, regardless of nominal capacity. This reflects a breakdown in the relationship between liquidity and timing of obligations. Capacity failure occurs when income is insufficient relative to load, eliminating the system's ability to sustain operations without structural change. Structural failure occurs when the relationships between components—income, expenses, liquidity, and exposure—no longer support stable operation, even if individual components continue to function in isolation.

These failure points are not independent. They interact. Liquidity depletion increases sensitivity to income variability. Reduced income capacity increases pressure on liquidity. Increased exposure amplifies the impact of both. The system moves toward failure as these relationships compress simultaneously. The specific failure point that is reached first depends on the structure of the system, but the progression toward that point follows a common pattern of increasing constraint and decreasing flexibility.

Systems do not fail at the moment of stress. They fail when stress exceeds structure.

This distinction is critical. Stress introduces constraint, but failure occurs when the system's structure cannot sustain operation under that constraint. A system with sufficient buffers and adaptable control processes may operate under significant stress without failing. A system with limited buffers and rigid structure may fail under relatively modest stress. The determining factor is not the presence of stress, but the relationship between stress and system structure.

The final function of the Governance Under Stress Mechanism is to reveal structure. Stress does not create dependencies, concentration, or rigidity. It exposes them. Under stable conditions, these characteristics may remain hidden because they do not produce immediate consequences. Under stress, they become visible because the system is forced to operate without excess capacity. Dependency concentration becomes apparent when a single failure disrupts the system. Buffer insufficiency becomes apparent when variation cannot be absorbed. Control effectiveness becomes apparent when adjustment either restores alignment or fails to do so under constraint.

Systems that appear stable under normal conditions may fail under stress because their structure relies on conditions that no longer hold. Systems that appear variable under normal conditions may remain stable under stress because their structure can absorb variation even when capacity is reduced. The difference lies in how the system is constructed, not how it appears during periods of low constraint.

Stress therefore serves as a revealing condition. It shows whether the system's structure is sufficient to maintain alignment when variation cannot be absorbed passively. It shows how buffers function when they are actively used. It shows how control processes operate when options are limited and timing is compressed. It shows where failure points exist and how close the system is to those points.

The Governance Under Stress Mechanism does not change how the system is structured. It exposes how the system behaves under constraint. This exposure defines the true condition of the system, independent of its performance under stable conditions.

The Simplicity Control Mechanism

The Simplicity Control Mechanism defines how reducing the number of interacting variables within a financial system increases clarity, improves interpretability, and enhances the effectiveness of control processes, resulting in greater stability over time. A financial system is not defined solely by its components, but by the relationships between those components and the pathways through which they interact. Each component—income streams, expense structures, liquidity layers, exposure channels—introduces variables. Each relationship between those components introduces interaction pathways. Each pathway increases the number of possible system states. As the number of variables and pathways expands, the system does not simply become larger. It becomes more complex in how it behaves, how it is observed, and how it is controlled.

Control depends on the ability to observe system state, interpret that state accurately, and apply adjustments that produce predictable outcomes. These functions rely on clarity. Clarity requires that cause and effect relationships can be identified with sufficient precision to allow accurate classification of signals and effective response. As the number of interacting variables increases, this clarity declines. The system becomes more difficult to track because changes in one component propagate through multiple pathways. Effects are distributed rather than localized. A single signal may reflect multiple underlying causes. A single adjustment may produce multiple downstream effects. This expansion of interaction increases the number of possible interpretations and reduces the reliability of any single interpretation.

Fewer variables produce a different structure. In a system with a limited number of components and interaction pathways, relationships remain direct. Changes in one component produce effects that can be traced with fewer intermediate steps. Observation captures a more accurate representation of system state because there are fewer overlapping influences. Interpretation becomes more reliable because signals map more directly to causes. Adjustment becomes more predictable because the number of interaction pathways through which that adjustment propagates is limited. The system remains fully functional, but its behavior is more transparent.

Control effectiveness declines as the number of interacting variables increases.

This decline does not occur because additional variables are inherently destabilizing. It occurs because each variable introduces additional uncertainty into the mapping between observation and action. When a signal is observed in a complex system, it may originate from multiple interacting components. The interpretation process must determine which of those components is responsible and how they interact. As the number of possible pathways increases, the probability of misclassification increases. Even if classification is accurate, the selection of an appropriate adjustment becomes more difficult because the adjustment will propagate through multiple pathways, producing effects that may not be fully predictable.

In a simpler system, the same signal can be interpreted with greater confidence. The number of potential causes is reduced, and the relationships between components are more transparent. This does not eliminate uncertainty, but it constrains it. The system's behavior becomes more legible. Legibility allows the control process to operate with higher precision because it can rely on a more accurate mapping between signals and underlying conditions.

Interpretation depends on clarity of relationships and visibility of cause and effect. In a system with fewer variables, these relationships are more visible. A change in liquidity relative to obligations can be observed and interpreted without being obscured by multiple overlapping factors. A shift in expense structure can be traced more directly to its impact on system load. A change in income behavior can be evaluated with fewer confounding variables. The signal remains connected to its source.

In a system with greater complexity, signals lose this direct mapping. A decline in liquidity may result from changes in income timing, expense variability, exposure shifts, or interactions between them. The interpretation process must account for all possible sources. This introduces ambiguity. Multiple explanations become plausible, and the selection of a single explanation becomes less certain. As ambiguity increases, the risk of misinterpretation increases. Misinterpretation leads to incorrect classification of system state and therefore incorrect adjustment.

Simplicity reduces ambiguity, improving the accuracy of classification and response.

This relationship connects directly to the mechanisms governing interpretation and complexity. When complexity increases, misinterpretation risk rises because signals are less clearly associated with their causes. Overlapping dependencies obscure the origin of variation. Hidden interactions produce outcomes that are not immediately attributable to a single source. The system may remain measurable, but the meaning of that measurement becomes less certain. As a result, the control process operates with reduced accuracy even if measurement itself remains intact.

Reducing the number of interacting variables reverses this effect. It does not eliminate variation or uncertainty, but it reduces the number of competing explanations for observed signals. This increases the probability that interpretation aligns with actual system conditions. When interpretation improves, the subsequent steps in the control loop—threshold evaluation and adjustment—operate on a more accurate foundation. The entire control process becomes more reliable because its inputs are clearer.

This clarity also affects the speed and effectiveness of adjustment cycles. Adjustment requires identifying deviation, selecting an appropriate response, and applying that response in a way that restores alignment. Each of these steps is influenced by the structure of the system. In a system with fewer variables, deviation can be identified more quickly because signals are less ambiguous. Response selection is more straightforward because there are fewer interacting components to consider. Application of the response is more direct because there are fewer pathways through which the adjustment must propagate.

In a more complex system, each step becomes slower and less certain. Identification of deviation requires more extensive interpretation because signals may originate from multiple sources. Response selection requires evaluation of how an adjustment will affect multiple interacting components. Application of the response produces effects that propagate through multiple layers, making the outcome less predictable. This increases the time between detection and effective correction. It also increases the likelihood that the adjustment will not fully restore alignment, requiring additional intervention.

Simpler systems reduce the delay between detection and effective correction.

This reduction in delay is not a function of increased speed alone. It reflects improved alignment between observation, interpretation, and adjustment. The control loop operates more efficiently because each stage is supported by clearer information and more predictable relationships.

The result is not simply faster response, but more effective response within the time available.

Simplicity therefore functions as a structural advantage in maintaining stability. Stability depends on clarity, predictability, and controllability. Clarity ensures that system state can be accurately observed and interpreted. Predictability ensures that adjustments produce expected outcomes. Controllability ensures that the system can be repositioned within its stability range using available actions. Each of these elements is strengthened when the number of interacting variables is reduced.

A complex system may offer greater capability in terms of the number of possible configurations and responses. However, this capability comes with reduced controllability. As the number of variables increases, the system becomes more difficult to interpret and adjust with precision. A simpler system offers fewer pathways, but those pathways are more transparent. This transparency allows control processes to operate with greater reliability. The system may have fewer options, but the outcomes of those options are more predictable. This predictability supports stable operation over time.

Simplicity does not reduce capability. It increases the reliability of control.

This reliability is critical under conditions of variability and stress. When variation increases, the system must rely on its control processes to maintain alignment. If those processes operate on ambiguous information or produce unpredictable outcomes, stability cannot be maintained. A system with greater structural simplicity retains clearer relationships under these conditions. Signals remain interpretable, and adjustments remain effective. This allows the system to operate within its stability range even as conditions change.

The interaction between simplicity and control becomes most apparent when considered in relation to the full control loop. Measurement provides data about system state. Detection identifies deviation.

Thresholds determine when action is required. Adjustment repositions the system. Each of these steps depends on the clarity of system structure. Measurement must capture meaningful data. Detection must classify that data accurately. Thresholds must be applied to signals that are correctly interpreted. Adjustment must produce predictable changes in system position. If the structure is too complex, each of these steps degrades. Measurement may capture data that is difficult to interpret. Detection may misclassify variation. Thresholds may be applied to signals that do not reflect underlying conditions. Adjustment may produce unintended consequences through multiple interaction pathways.

Control requires clarity because stability depends on the ability to interpret and adjust system behavior accurately.

This relationship defines the role of the Simplicity Control Mechanism within the broader system of governance. It does not eliminate the need for measurement, detection, thresholds, or adjustment. It supports these mechanisms by preserving the clarity required for them to function effectively. By reducing the number of interacting variables, the system maintains a structure that can be observed, understood, and controlled with greater precision. This increases the reliability of the control process and therefore the stability of the system over time.

The mechanism does not operate by removing all complexity. Financial systems inherently contain multiple components and interactions. The mechanism operates by limiting unnecessary complexity—interactions that do not contribute to system function but increase ambiguity and reduce controllability. By constraining the number of variables and pathways, the system maintains a structure that can be governed effectively under both stable and stressed conditions.

The result is not a system that avoids variation or change. It is a system that can respond to variation and change with greater accuracy and reliability. Stability is not achieved by eliminating movement, but by maintaining control over that movement. Simplicity enhances that control by preserving the clarity required for effective governance.

Governance & Liquidity Mechanism

The Governance & Liquidity Mechanism defines how a financial system monitors, interprets, and maintains its liquidity position over time, ensuring that sufficient temporal capacity exists to sustain operation under variability and constraint. Liquidity is not a static reserve measured solely by balance. It is a continuously shifting measure of time—the duration the system can continue operating given its current configuration of inflow, outflow, and buffer structure. Governance operates on this temporal dimension. It does not simply observe how much liquidity exists. It determines how long the system can remain viable under present conditions and how that duration is changing.

Liquidity therefore functions as the interface between system position and time-to-failure. All other system relationships—income relative to expenses, exposure relative to tolerance, capacity relative to load—ultimately converge into a single constraint: how long the system can sustain those relationships before they break. This duration is not fixed. It expands and contracts as system components evolve. Governance requires continuous visibility into this changing time horizon because the ability to respond to deviation depends on the amount of time available to respond.

Tracking liquidity position begins with reframing liquidity from a balance into a temporal state. A balance expresses quantity at a point in time. A temporal state expresses duration across time. The same balance produces different runway depending on the structure of the system in which it operates. A given level of liquidity may represent extended operational capacity under low expense load and stable inflow, or minimal capacity under high load and volatile inflow. The balance alone does not define stability. The relationship between liquidity and system demands defines how long stability can be maintained.

Liquidity position must therefore be evaluated relative to expense load, income variability, and obligation timing. Expense load determines the rate at which liquidity is consumed. Income variability determines the uncertainty of replenishment. Obligation timing determines when liquidity must be available, not simply how much is required in aggregate. These relationships transform liquidity from a static quantity into a dynamic measure of duration. Governance requires that these relationships be continuously observed, because changes in any of them alter the system's temporal capacity even if the nominal liquidity balance remains unchanged.

This continuous observation includes tracking absolute liquidity levels, the rate at which those levels are changing, and the variability in inflow and outflow timing. A stable balance with increasing variability in expenses produces a different liquidity position than a declining balance with stable expenses. A system in which inflows arrive irregularly requires different temporal interpretation than one with consistent inflow timing. Liquidity position is therefore not a single value. It is a state defined by multiple interacting dimensions that together determine how long the system can operate.

Liquidity must be interpreted in terms of time, not amount.

This interpretation becomes critical when considering runway degradation. Runway represents the duration the system can continue operating under current conditions. It is not lost at a single moment. It compresses progressively as conditions change. This compression occurs through multiple pathways. Liquidity may decline directly through consumption. Expense load may increase, accelerating the rate of consumption. Income reliability may weaken, reducing the certainty of replenishment. Variability may increase, introducing greater dispersion in outcomes. Each of these factors reduces the duration over which the system can sustain itself.

The rate at which runway degrades is as significant as the level of runway itself. A slow decline allows for adjustment because the system retains sufficient time to interpret signals and apply corrective action. An accelerating decline compresses the time available for response. As runway shortens, the system becomes more sensitive to variation. Small changes in inflow or outflow produce larger proportional effects on remaining duration. This sensitivity increases as runway approaches its lower bounds. The system does not simply have less time. It has less capacity to absorb additional variation within that time.

Runway defines the system's margin for correction.

This margin determines whether the control loop can function effectively. When runway is extended, the system can tolerate delays in detection, minor misinterpretations, and incremental adjustments. When runway compresses, these tolerances narrow. Detection must occur earlier relative to deviation. Interpretation must be more accurate because errors consume a larger proportion of remaining time. Adjustment must be more precise because misalignment reduces already limited capacity. The control loop does not disappear under reduced runway. It becomes more constrained, operating within tighter temporal limits.

Buffer awareness defines how this temporal capacity is structured and how it can be utilized. Buffers include liquidity reserves, flexible expense structures, and excess capacity within the system. These buffers determine not only how much runway exists, but how that runway can be deployed. A nominal buffer may exist in the system but may not be accessible when required. Liquidity held in illiquid form does not extend usable runway under time constraint. Expenses that appear adjustable may be structurally rigid in the relevant time frame. Capacity that exists under normal conditions may not be available under stress.

Buffer awareness requires understanding the size, accessibility, and burn rate of these buffers. Size determines the potential extension of runway. Accessibility determines whether that extension can be realized when needed. Burn rate determines how quickly the buffer is consumed once deployed. These dimensions must be considered together. A large buffer with low accessibility provides less functional runway than a smaller buffer that can be deployed immediately. A buffer with a high burn rate provides limited duration even if its nominal size appears sufficient.

The distinction between nominal and usable buffer defines hidden fragility. Systems may appear stable based on nominal buffer levels, but if those buffers cannot be accessed or deployed effectively, the system's actual temporal capacity is significantly lower than assumed. This misalignment between perceived and actual runway reduces the effectiveness of the control loop because decisions are made under incorrect assumptions about available time. Buffer awareness aligns perception with functional capacity, ensuring that governance operates on accurate temporal information.

Buffers determine how long the system can remain stable under pressure.

This determination connects directly to the integration of liquidity within the control loop. Liquidity functions as a primary signal input because it translates system configuration into time. Detection mechanisms identify changes in runway. Thresholds define minimum acceptable durations. Adjustment processes operate to preserve or extend runway when those thresholds are approached. Liquidity therefore informs each stage of the control loop by providing a temporal reference for system state.

As liquidity compresses, it affects more than the level of available resources. It compresses decision time, reduces margin for error, and limits the flexibility of response. When runway is extended, the system can evaluate multiple response pathways and absorb minor inefficiencies. When runway is short, the range of viable responses narrows. Decisions must be made with less information and less tolerance for error. This does not eliminate governance. It intensifies the constraints under which governance operates.

The function of governance within this mechanism is to maintain runway before crisis conditions emerge. This requires that liquidity be monitored and interpreted continuously, not only when it approaches critical levels. If monitoring is absent or delayed, runway degradation may proceed without detection. If interpretation is incorrect, the rate or significance of degradation may be misclassified. If adjustment is misaligned, liquidity may be consumed inefficiently, accelerating the compression of runway. Each of these failures reduces the time available for response and increases the probability that the system will reach its failure boundary without effective intervention.

Liquidity converts system state into time for action.

This conversion makes liquidity central to the system's ability to remain stable under variability. Other system properties—income stability, expense control, exposure management—define the structure within which the system operates. Liquidity defines how long that structure can sustain operation when those properties are under pressure. It is the mechanism through which capacity becomes duration and through which duration enables control.

The dynamics of this mechanism evolve over time. In early stages, liquidity is stable or increasing, and runway is extended. The system operates with substantial temporal capacity, and monitoring may exist without urgency. Buffer awareness may be low because the system is not operating near its constraints. Variation can be absorbed without immediate consequence, and the control loop operates with wide tolerances.

In mid-stage conditions, runway begins to compress. Liquidity variability increases, and the relationship between inflow and outflow becomes less stable. Monitoring becomes more active because changes in liquidity position have more immediate implications for system stability. Buffer awareness becomes necessary because the system must understand not only how much capacity exists, but how that capacity can be deployed. The control loop operates with narrower tolerances, requiring more accurate detection and interpretation.

In late-stage conditions, runway is short and highly sensitive. Small changes in system inputs produce significant changes in remaining duration. The control loop operates under time pressure, with limited margin for error. Liquidity dominates system behavior because it defines the immediate boundary between continued operation and failure. At this stage, the system's ability to maintain stability depends almost entirely on its remaining temporal capacity and the effectiveness with which that capacity is managed.

Failure within this mechanism occurs when liquidity position is not actively monitored, when runway degradation is not detected or is misinterpreted, when buffers are assumed rather than verified, or when the control loop operates without awareness of temporal constraint. Under these conditions, the system continues to function without recognizing that its capacity to sustain operation is diminishing. Deviation may be detected in other system components, but without an accurate understanding of available time, adjustments may be delayed, misaligned, or insufficient.

The result is a loss of the system's ability to respond before reaching its failure boundary. Instability does not emerge from a single shock event. It emerges from the absence of temporal capacity required to absorb variation and apply correction. The system does not fail because it lacks resources in absolute terms. It fails because it lacks the time required to deploy those resources effectively within the constraints imposed by its structure.

Liquidity defines how long a system can remain viable under its current configuration.

Governance requires maintaining that time.

Governance & Income Mechanism

The Governance & Income Mechanism defines how a financial system monitors, interprets, and maintains the stability of its inflows over time, ensuring that variability in income does not disrupt alignment between capacity and system load. Income is not a fixed input. It is a variable flow that changes in magnitude, timing, and reliability. Governance operates by continuously observing these variations, converting them into signals, and integrating those signals into the control process so that system positioning remains aligned with available capacity.

Income functions as the primary input that defines the system's capacity to sustain its obligations. While liquidity determines how long the system can operate under constraint, income determines the rate at which capacity is replenished. The interaction between income and expenses defines whether the system accumulates capacity, maintains equilibrium, or depletes its reserves. Because income is inherently variable, the system must treat it not as a constant foundation but as a fluctuating input whose behavior over time determines the stability of the entire structure.

Monitoring income variability begins with the recognition that income exists as a flow, not a fixed value. This flow is characterized by three dimensions: magnitude, timing, and reliability. Magnitude reflects the amount received within a given period. Timing reflects when that amount is received relative to obligations. Reliability reflects the consistency of these patterns across time. Each dimension influences how income contributes to system stability. A stable magnitude with irregular timing produces a different capacity profile than a variable magnitude with consistent timing. Reliability determines whether observed patterns can be used to anticipate future capacity or must be treated as uncertain inputs.

Monitoring requires tracking these dimensions as patterns rather than isolated events. A single period of reduced income does not define system behavior. It must be evaluated relative to prior periods to determine whether it represents normal variability or a shift in underlying structure. Similarly, an increase in income magnitude does not necessarily indicate improved stability if it is accompanied by increased volatility or irregular timing. Governance requires observing how income behaves across sequences, identifying patterns that define its structure, and detecting when those patterns begin to change.

The distinction between stable and variable income is not binary. All income contains some degree of variability. The relevant distinction lies between predictable variability and irregular variability. Predictable variability follows patterns that can be incorporated into system expectations. Irregular variability introduces uncertainty that must be absorbed through buffers or flexibility. Variability itself is not destabilizing. It becomes destabilizing when it exceeds the system's tolerance to absorb it without altering alignment between capacity and load.

Higher variability increases the demands placed on the system. It requires greater liquidity buffers to absorb fluctuations, greater flexibility in expense structure to accommodate timing differences, and more responsive governance processes to interpret changes. Lower variability allows the system to operate with tighter configuration because capacity is more predictable. These relationships define how income variability interacts with system structure. The same level of variability produces different stability outcomes depending on the system's ability to absorb it.

Income must therefore be monitored as a pattern over time, not as discrete receipts.

Signals emerge when income behavior deviates from its expected pattern. These signals represent changes in magnitude, timing, or reliability that may affect system capacity. A sustained reduction in magnitude indicates a potential decrease in available capacity. A disruption in timing indicates that capacity may not be available when required, even if total income remains unchanged. A breakdown in reliability indicates that future inflows cannot be anticipated with the same level of confidence, increasing uncertainty within the system.

Detection of these signals requires distinguishing between noise and meaningful change. Income flows naturally exhibit variation from period to period. This variation may reflect normal fluctuations rather than structural shifts. Detection mechanisms must evaluate persistence and impact. A temporary deviation that resolves within expected patterns does not represent a meaningful signal. A deviation that persists across multiple periods or alters the relationship between income and expenses indicates a change that may require adjustment.

This classification interacts directly with prior mechanisms. Misinterpretation can lead to incorrect classification of income signals, causing the system to respond to temporary variation as if it were structural or to ignore structural change as if it were temporary. Overreaction can result from responding to short-term variability without confirming its persistence or impact. Neglect can allow gradual degradation in income stability to go undetected, particularly when variability increases slowly over time. Each of these failures distorts the system's ability to interpret income behavior accurately.

The significance of income signals is defined by their effect on system relationships. A change in income magnitude becomes meaningful when it alters the balance between capacity and load. A timing disruption becomes meaningful when it affects the system's ability to meet obligations without drawing on liquidity. A reliability breakdown becomes meaningful when it reduces the predictability required for effective planning and control.

Signals are not evaluated in isolation. They are evaluated in terms of how they affect the system's ability to maintain alignment.

Income signals must be classified before they inform adjustment.

Adjustment triggers are not activated by income change alone. They are activated when income variation alters system relationships in a way that affects stability. A reduction in income magnitude does not necessarily require adjustment if it remains within the system's tolerance. A temporary delay in income may not require adjustment if liquidity buffers can absorb the timing difference. Triggers are defined by thresholds that represent the limits of acceptable variation within the system.

These thresholds are tied to capacity relative to load and to the interaction between income and liquidity. A sustained reduction in inflow magnitude that compresses capacity below required levels triggers adjustment because it alters the system's ability to sustain its obligations. Increased variability that exceeds tolerance triggers adjustment because it introduces uncertainty that cannot be absorbed without structural change. A breakdown in timing consistency triggers adjustment when it disrupts the synchronization between inflow and outflow. Reduced reliability triggers adjustment when it undermines the predictability required to maintain alignment.

The timing of these triggers determines the scale and nature of adjustment. Early detection allows for incremental changes that preserve alignment without significant disruption. Delayed detection requires larger corrections because deviation has accumulated over time. The system does not respond to income variability at the moment it occurs. It responds when that variability crosses thresholds that define its impact on stability.

Adjustment pathways operate at the structural level. They modify relationships within the system rather than reacting to individual income events. Changes in expense structure alter the load relative to capacity. Adjustments in liquidity positioning alter the buffer available to absorb variability. Rebalancing exposure dependencies alters the system's sensitivity to changes in income. These adjustments are not tactical responses to individual fluctuations. They are structural responses to changes in the pattern of income behavior.

Income changes require response only when they alter system stability.

The dynamics of this mechanism evolve through distinct stages. In early-stage conditions, income remains stable or varies within expected patterns. Signals are minimal or transient, and the system absorbs variation without requiring adjustment. Monitoring remains active, but its role is primarily confirmatory. The system operates with sufficient tolerance to accommodate normal fluctuations.

In mid-stage conditions, variability increases or patterns begin to shift. Signals become more frequent or more persistent. Detection becomes more critical because the distinction between temporary and structural change becomes less clear. The system begins to approach its tolerance limits, and adjustment triggers may activate as relationships between capacity and load begin to shift. Monitoring transitions from passive observation to active interpretation.

In late-stage conditions, income instability becomes sustained. Reliability declines, and patterns that previously defined system behavior no longer hold. Signals become continuous rather than intermittent, indicating structural change rather than temporary variation. The system must adjust its configuration to maintain alignment because the prior structure is no longer compatible with the new behavior of income. At this stage, the mechanism shifts from maintaining stability within an existing structure to supporting adaptation of the structure itself.

Failure within this mechanism occurs when income variability is not monitored as a pattern, when signals are misclassified or ignored, when temporary changes are treated as structural or structural changes are treated as temporary, and when adjustment triggers are delayed or misaligned. Under these conditions, the system continues to operate under incorrect assumptions about its capacity. Expenses remain aligned to a level of income that no longer exists, or liquidity absorbs variability until it is depleted.

This failure does not occur as a sudden event. It develops as a progressive misalignment between capacity and load. Income variability introduces changes that are not correctly interpreted, leading to delayed or incorrect adjustments. Liquidity temporarily absorbs the resulting imbalance, masking the underlying misalignment. As variability persists, liquidity is consumed, compressing runway and reducing the system's ability to respond. Eventually, the system reaches a point where capacity is insufficient to sustain its obligations, and instability emerges.

The system does not fail because income changes. It fails because income changes are not correctly interpreted and integrated into the control process.

Income defines the system's capacity.

Governance requires maintaining the stability of that capacity as it changes.

Governance & Expense Mechanism

The Governance & Expense Mechanism defines how a financial system monitors, interprets, and controls its outflows over time, ensuring that expense behavior remains aligned with system capacity and does not introduce structural drift. Expenses are not static obligations. They are dynamic expressions of system load that evolve in level, structure, and flexibility. Governance operates by continuously observing these changes, classifying their significance, and maintaining alignment between load and capacity as conditions shift.

Expenses represent the demand side of the system. While income defines capacity and liquidity defines time, expenses define the rate at which capacity is consumed. Stability depends on maintaining a consistent relationship between these elements. When expenses evolve without coordination, that relationship begins to degrade. This degradation does not typically occur through abrupt shifts. It emerges through gradual, incremental changes that accumulate over time. The mechanism of governance must therefore operate continuously, detecting these changes as they develop rather than reacting after they have been embedded into the system.

Expense drift is the primary form through which this misalignment develops. Drift is defined as the gradual, uncoordinated increase or structural shift in outflows that occurs without a corresponding adjustment in system capacity. It is not a single event. It is the cumulative effect of repeated small changes that individually appear insignificant but collectively alter the system's load profile. These changes may occur across multiple categories, each contributing a marginal increase that remains below detection thresholds when evaluated in isolation.

The characteristics of drift make it difficult to identify at the point of occurrence. Changes are incremental rather than discrete. They accumulate across time rather than appearing as a single deviation. Visibility is low because each individual adjustment falls within expected variation. The system continues to function, and no immediate threshold is breached. However, the aggregate effect of these changes gradually increases the baseline level of expenses, shifting the system's load without triggering immediate corrective action.

Understanding drift requires analyzing expenses across three dimensions: level, structure, and variability. Level represents total outflow over a given period. Structure represents the composition of that outflow, including the balance between fixed and flexible components. Variability represents the consistency of expenses across time. A change in any of these dimensions can alter the system's load profile. An increase in level raises total demand on capacity. A shift toward more fixed expenses reduces flexibility. Increased variability introduces uncertainty in outflow timing and magnitude.

Detection of drift requires tracking patterns across periods rather than evaluating individual transactions. The system must identify deviations from its established baseline structure, recognizing when incremental changes begin to accumulate into a meaningful shift. This involves distinguishing between intentional changes—those aligned with system design—and unobserved accumulation, which occurs without coordinated adjustment. Intentional changes reflect deliberate modification of system structure. Unobserved accumulation reflects passive evolution that gradually alters load without explicit recognition.

Drift is not event-based. It emerges from repeated small adjustments.

This distinction is critical because event-based detection mechanisms are not effective against gradual accumulation. Systems designed to respond to discrete deviations may fail to identify drift until it has progressed to a point where significant correction is required. Governance must therefore operate with sensitivity to incremental change, recognizing that stability can erode without any single observable event marking the transition.

Expenses must be monitored as an evolving structure, not as fixed commitments.

Within this evolving structure, leakage represents a distinct form of misalignment. Leakage is defined as outflows that do not correspond to intentional system structure. Unlike drift, which alters the baseline through coordinated or semi-coordinated changes, leakage consists of unstructured expenditures that accumulate without contributing to system function. These outflows are typically distributed across multiple categories, each with low individual magnitude but significant cumulative impact.

The characteristics of leakage make it difficult to isolate. Individual components appear insignificant, often falling within normal variation. However, their cumulative effect reduces effective capacity by increasing total load without providing structural benefit. Leakage differs from drift in that it does not necessarily shift the baseline structure in a coordinated way. Instead, it introduces inefficiency into the system by allowing resources to be consumed without contributing to stability or function.

Sources of leakage include untracked variability, overlapping or redundant expenses, and the persistence of outdated commitments that no longer align with system requirements. These sources often remain undetected because they do not produce clear signals when evaluated individually. Detection requires visibility into total system outflows and comparison between intended structure and actual behavior. The system must identify which outflows serve a functional role and which do not, recognizing that misalignment can exist even when overall expense levels appear stable.

Leakage impacts the system by reducing effective capacity, accelerating liquidity consumption, and distorting the relationship between load and income. Because leakage operates without clear signals, it degrades alignment without triggering immediate corrective action. The system continues to function, but with reduced efficiency and increased vulnerability to variability. Over time, this degradation contributes to instability by narrowing the margin between capacity and load.

Unstructured outflows degrade system alignment without clear signals.

Control of expenses is achieved through monitoring, which functions as the primary mechanism for maintaining alignment. Monitoring provides the visibility required to detect drift and identify leakage. Without visibility, classification is not possible, and without classification, correction cannot occur. Monitoring does not eliminate expenses. It maintains alignment between load and capacity by ensuring that changes in expense behavior are observed, interpreted, and integrated into the control process.

Effective monitoring requires sufficient frequency to detect drift before it becomes embedded in the system. If monitoring intervals are too long, incremental changes accumulate without detection, increasing the scale of adjustment required when misalignment becomes visible. Monitoring must also be consistent across categories, ensuring that all components of the expense structure are observed. Inconsistent monitoring creates blind spots where drift and leakage can develop without detection.

Integration with income and liquidity signals is essential because expenses do not operate independently. Changes in expense behavior must be evaluated relative to changes in capacity and temporal constraints. An increase in expenses may be sustainable if income and liquidity provide sufficient support. The same increase may produce instability if capacity is constrained or if liquidity is limited. Monitoring must therefore operate within the context of the entire system, not as an isolated process.

Within the control loop, monitoring captures outflow patterns, detection identifies deviations from baseline structure, thresholds define acceptable load relative to capacity, and adjustment modifies structure when thresholds are exceeded. Each stage depends on the quality of monitoring. If monitoring fails, detection is delayed or inaccurate. If detection fails, thresholds are not evaluated correctly. If thresholds are misapplied, adjustment becomes misaligned. The effectiveness of the entire control loop depends on continuous visibility into expense behavior.

Monitoring failure leads to delayed awareness, accumulated drift, and increased reliance on large corrections. When drift is not detected early, it becomes embedded in the system's baseline, requiring more significant adjustments to restore alignment. When leakage is not identified, it continues to consume capacity, reducing the system's ability to absorb variation. These effects compound over time, increasing the system's vulnerability to instability.

Control of expenses is achieved through continuous visibility and classification.

The dynamics of this mechanism evolve through stages that reflect the progression of expense behavior. In early-stage conditions, the expense structure is stable, and variability remains within expected bounds. Drift is minimal or absent, and leakage is limited. Monitoring remains active but operates with low urgency because the system is not approaching its constraints. The relationship between load and capacity remains aligned, and the system can absorb normal variation without requiring adjustment.

In mid-stage conditions, gradual drift begins to emerge. Incremental changes accumulate across categories, and leakage becomes detectable as unstructured outflows increase. Variability may rise, introducing greater dispersion in expense patterns. Monitoring becomes more critical because the distinction between normal variation and meaningful deviation becomes less clear. Detection must identify whether changes represent temporary fluctuations or structural shifts. Adjustment may begin to occur as thresholds are approached, but the system still retains sufficient flexibility to respond incrementally.

In late-stage conditions, the expense structure becomes misaligned with capacity. Drift is embedded in the baseline, and leakage has accumulated into a meaningful component of total load. Variability may be elevated, further complicating interpretation. Adjustment becomes necessary to restore alignment because the system can no longer sustain its current configuration. At this stage, the scale of correction required is larger because misalignment has developed over an extended period without adequate intervention.

Failure within this mechanism occurs when expense drift is not detected, leakage is not identified or is ignored, monitoring is inconsistent or absent, and expense structure evolves without coordination. Under these conditions, load increases relative to capacity without corresponding adjustment. The system continues to operate, but with a progressively narrowing margin between inflow and outflow.

Liquidity absorbs this imbalance temporarily, masking the underlying misalignment. As expenses increase relative to income, liquidity is consumed to maintain operation. This consumption reduces runway, compressing the time available for response. The system does not immediately fail because liquidity provides a buffer. However, as that buffer is depleted, the system approaches its failure boundary. When liquidity is no longer sufficient to absorb the imbalance, instability emerges as outflows exceed sustainable levels.

This process does not depend on a single triggering event. It is the result of progressive misalignment between load and capacity. Drift increases baseline expenses. Leakage introduces inefficiency. Monitoring failure delays detection. Adjustment is delayed or insufficient. Liquidity absorbs the imbalance until it can no longer do so. The system reaches a point where it cannot sustain its obligations, and failure occurs as a consequence of accumulated deviation.

Expenses define the system's load.

Governance requires maintaining control over that load as it evolves.

Governance & Risk Mechanism

The Governance & Risk Mechanism defines how a financial system continuously monitors, interprets, and manages exposure to uncertainty, ensuring that risk remains aligned with system tolerance and does not accumulate into instability. Risk is not a discrete event. It is a continuous condition embedded within the structure of the system. Exposure exists regardless of whether disruption occurs. Governance operates by maintaining alignment between that exposure and the system's capacity to absorb variation.

Exposure represents the system's sensitivity to change. It determines how variation in income, expenses, liquidity, or external conditions translates into impact. This sensitivity is not fixed. It evolves as the relationships between system components change. A system with stable income, flexible expenses, and deep liquidity exhibits low sensitivity to variation. A system with concentrated income, rigid expenses, and limited liquidity exhibits high sensitivity. Governance requires continuous awareness of this sensitivity because stability depends not on the absence of variation, but on the system's ability to absorb it.

Exposure must therefore be monitored as an evolving condition. It is not sufficient to evaluate risk at a single point in time. The system's structure changes continuously, altering the way it responds to variation. Income sources may become more concentrated. Expenses may become more rigid. Liquidity may be reduced or constrained. Each of these changes increases exposure by altering the system's sensitivity to disruption. These changes often occur without discrete events. They emerge through gradual shifts in system configuration.

Exposure exists in multiple forms. Concentration increases exposure by reducing diversification across income sources or obligations. Dependency increases exposure by linking system performance to specific components whose failure would produce disproportionate impact. Sensitivity increases exposure by amplifying the effect of variation, particularly when margins are compressed. These forms of exposure are not external to the system. They are embedded within its structure, shaped by the relationships between income, expenses, liquidity, and obligations.

Monitoring exposure requires observing these relationships over time. It involves identifying how concentration changes, how dependencies develop, and how sensitivity increases or decreases as conditions evolve. This monitoring cannot rely on isolated measurements. It must evaluate patterns across periods, recognizing that exposure accumulates through incremental changes. The system may appear stable when evaluated at a single point, but underlying exposure may be increasing as structural relationships shift.

Exposure changes continuously as system relationships evolve, requiring continuous monitoring to maintain visibility into risk position.

Within this continuous evolution, risk drift represents the primary mechanism through which exposure increases without detection. Risk drift is defined as the gradual accumulation of exposure over time without discrete triggering events. Unlike shocks, which produce immediate and visible effects, drift operates incrementally. Each change contributes a small increase in exposure that may not be significant in isolation but becomes meaningful when aggregated across time.

Sources of risk drift are embedded in the structure of the system. Concentration may increase as income becomes reliant on fewer sources. Redundancy may decline as alternative pathways are removed or allowed to lapse. Dependency chains may expand, linking system performance to additional conditions that must hold for stability to persist. Margins may tighten as expenses increase relative to income or as liquidity is reduced. Each of these changes increases exposure, but none necessarily produces a discrete signal indicating that risk has increased.

The characteristics of drift make it difficult to detect. It is incremental rather than discrete. It accumulates gradually. It operates with low visibility because each individual change falls within expected variation. Traditional detection mechanisms rely on threshold breaches or sudden deviations. Drift does not produce such signals. It moves the system toward instability without triggering immediate recognition.

The distinction between drift and shock is critical. Shock represents an external or internal event that produces a sudden change in system conditions. Drift represents a structural movement that alters the system's sensitivity to such events. A system with low exposure may absorb a shock without instability. A system with high exposure may fail under the same shock. The event does not determine the outcome. Exposure determines how the system responds.

Risk drift increases system vulnerability through gradual accumulation of exposure without discrete signals.

Because drift does not produce clear signals, governance must operate with sensitivity to structural change rather than relying solely on event-based detection. Failure to recognize drift allows exposure to accumulate until the system's tolerance is exceeded. At that point, even minor variation can produce disproportionate impact because the system's capacity to absorb change has been reduced.

System tolerance defines the boundary within which exposure can be absorbed without instability. Tolerance is not a subjective measure. It is determined by the system's structural capacity to absorb variation. This capacity is defined by liquidity depth, income stability, and expense flexibility. Liquidity provides time, allowing the system to absorb disruption without immediate failure. Income stability provides predictability, reducing variability in capacity. Expense flexibility allows load to adjust in response to changing conditions.

Exposure must be evaluated relative to this capacity. Risk does not exist in isolation. A given level of exposure may be sustainable in one system and destabilizing in another. A system with high liquidity and flexible expenses may tolerate higher exposure because it can absorb variation over time. A system with limited liquidity and rigid expenses may require lower exposure because it has less capacity to absorb disruption.

Misalignment occurs when exposure exceeds system tolerance. This misalignment may arise from underestimating exposure or overestimating tolerance. Underestimation occurs when the system fails to recognize how concentration, dependency, or sensitivity has increased. Overestimation occurs when the system assumes that its capacity to absorb variation is greater than it actually is. Both conditions produce the same outcome: exposure exceeds the system's ability to manage it.

When exposure exceeds tolerance, the system becomes fragile. Small variations produce disproportionately large effects because the margin for absorption has been reduced. Liquidity may temporarily absorb the impact, masking the underlying misalignment. However, this masking effect is temporary. As liquidity is consumed, the system approaches a point where it can no longer absorb variation. At that point, instability becomes visible.

Stability depends on maintaining exposure within system tolerance defined by capacity, liquidity, and structural flexibility.

Exposure functions as a critical input to the control loop. It informs how variation is interpreted and how thresholds are defined. Measurement captures changes in system structure, including shifts in concentration, dependency, and sensitivity. Detection identifies when these changes represent meaningful increases in exposure. Thresholds define acceptable levels of exposure relative to system tolerance. Adjustment modifies system configuration to restore alignment when thresholds are exceeded.

Risk signals emerge from changes in system relationships. An increase in concentration reduces diversification and increases exposure. An increase in dependency links system performance to additional conditions, amplifying sensitivity to failure. A reduction in margin reduces the system's ability to absorb variation. Each of these signals indicates a change in exposure that must be evaluated within the context of system tolerance.

Thresholds translate these signals into actionable boundaries. They define the level of exposure beyond which stability is compromised. These thresholds are not fixed. They depend on the system's capacity at a given point in time. As liquidity changes, as income stability shifts, and as expense flexibility evolves, the system's tolerance changes. Thresholds must therefore reflect current conditions rather than static assumptions.

Adjustment operates by modifying the structure of the system to realign exposure with tolerance. This may involve redistributing exposure, reducing concentration, or increasing buffers. These adjustments are not independent of other system components. Changes in exposure affect liquidity, income, and expenses. For example, reducing concentration in income sources may alter income variability. Increasing buffers affects liquidity and may require changes in expense structure. Governance must therefore integrate exposure management with the broader system.

Exposure informs control processes by defining how system variability translates into instability risk.

Failure dynamics emerge when exposure is not managed effectively. The progression toward failure follows a consistent pattern. Exposure increases through drift. This increase remains undetected or is misinterpreted. Monitoring fails to capture the change, or detection mechanisms do not classify it as significant. The system continues to operate under the assumption that its exposure remains within tolerance.

As exposure accumulates, the system becomes increasingly sensitive to variation. Liquidity may mask this sensitivity by absorbing fluctuations. However, this masking effect reduces runway, compressing the time available for response. Eventually, exposure exceeds tolerance. At this point, the system is structurally fragile, even if no visible instability has yet occurred.

Failure is triggered when variation interacts with this accumulated exposure. The triggering event may be minor relative to the system's prior experience. However, because exposure has increased, the system's response to that event is amplified. The event reveals the underlying fragility that has developed through drift. The system appears to fail suddenly, but the conditions for failure have been accumulating over time.

The distinction between exposure and event is critical. Exposure creates fragility. The event reveals it. Without exposure, the event may not produce instability. With exposure, even small variations can produce failure. Governance must therefore focus on managing exposure rather than predicting events. Stability depends on maintaining alignment between exposure and tolerance, not on anticipating specific disruptions.

Systems fail when accumulated exposure exceeds tolerance and variation reveals underlying structural fragility.

At the system level, risk governance determines whether stability can be maintained over time. Stable systems continuously align exposure with tolerance. They monitor changes in system structure, detect drift, and adjust configuration to maintain balance between sensitivity and capacity. Unstable systems allow exposure to accumulate without adjustment. They rely on the absence of events to maintain stability, rather than on structural alignment.

Risk is continuously present. It is not eliminated through management. Governance does not remove exposure. It maintains exposure within boundaries that the system can absorb. This requires continuous alignment across all system dimensions. Income defines capacity. Expenses define load. Liquidity defines time. Exposure defines sensitivity. Stability depends on maintaining coherence among these elements as conditions evolve.

Governance is therefore an ongoing process. It does not operate periodically. It does not respond only when instability becomes visible. It continuously evaluates system relationships, ensuring that exposure remains within tolerance. This evaluation must account for gradual changes as well as discrete events. It must integrate signals from all components of the system, recognizing that exposure is shaped by the interaction of income, expenses, and liquidity.

Stability is maintained by continuously aligning exposure with system tolerance as conditions evolve.

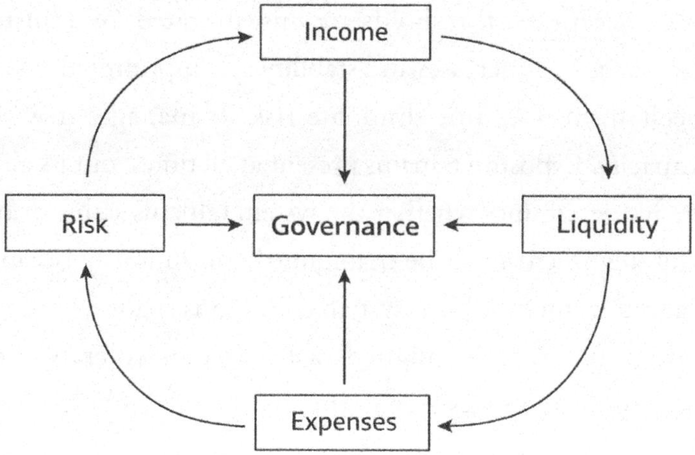

[Figure 9: Full Financial Governance System Map]

The system can be understood as a closed loop connecting four primary components: income, expenses, liquidity, and exposure. Income provides capacity. Expenses define load. Liquidity provides time. Exposure defines sensitivity. At the center of this system is governance, which monitors, interprets, and adjusts these components to maintain alignment.

Measurement captures changes in each component. Detection identifies deviations from expected patterns. Thresholds define acceptable ranges for each relationship. Adjustment modifies system configuration to restore alignment. These processes operate continuously, forming a feedback loop that maintains stability. Exposure integrates into this loop by defining how variation in any component translates into risk. Without this integration, the system cannot accurately assess its sensitivity to change.

The outer structure of the system is defined by this continuous loop of measurement, detection, threshold evaluation, and adjustment. Each component feeds into governance, and governance feeds back into each component. Stability emerges from the coherence of this loop. When any element of the loop fails—when measurement is incomplete, detection is inaccurate, thresholds are miscalibrated, or adjustment is misaligned—exposure increases and stability is compromised.

The mechanism does not eliminate risk. It manages it within the system's capacity. Exposure remains present at all times, but its alignment with tolerance determines whether the system remains stable or becomes fragile. This alignment must be maintained continuously because both exposure and tolerance evolve as system conditions change.

Exposure must remain aligned with system tolerance because unmanaged risk accumulates even in the absence of visible instability.

Stability Is Maintained, Not Achieved

Stability is commonly framed as an outcome. It is treated as a condition that can be reached through correct configuration, preserved through discipline, and retained through consistency of behavior. This framing assumes that once a system is properly constructed, it can remain aligned without continuous intervention. It implies that stability is a destination—a point at which variability no longer threatens system integrity.

This assumption fails because the system itself does not remain static. Income changes in magnitude, timing, and reliability. Expenses evolve in structure, level, and flexibility. Liquidity expands and contracts as buffers are built and consumed. Exposure shifts as dependencies, concentrations, and sensitivities change over time. Each component of the system moves continuously, altering the relationships that define alignment.

A static configuration cannot remain stable under continuous change. Even if alignment is achieved at a given point, the underlying conditions that supported that alignment will not persist unchanged. The system will move. Relationships will shift. Margins will compress or expand. Dependencies will strengthen or weaken. These changes occur regardless of whether they are observed or acknowledged.

Stability cannot exist as a fixed outcome because the system itself is continuously changing.

This continuous movement establishes the requirement for governance. Governance is not triggered by instability. It is not a response mechanism activated only when deviation becomes visible. It is the ongoing process through which the system is observed, interpreted, and adjusted in response to continuous change. Without governance, the system does not remain stable. It continues to operate, but its alignment degrades as underlying relationships shift.

Monitoring provides visibility into system behavior. It captures changes in income patterns, expense structure, liquidity position, and exposure dynamics. Evaluation interprets these changes, determining whether they represent normal variability or meaningful deviation. Adjustment modifies system configuration to maintain alignment within acceptable bounds. These processes do not occur intermittently. They operate continuously because the system they govern is continuously evolving.

In the absence of governance, drift becomes the dominant mechanism. Income variability may increase without recognition. Expenses may gradually expand or become more rigid. Liquidity may decline or become less accessible. Exposure may accumulate through concentration or dependency. Each of these changes alters system relationships, but without monitoring and evaluation, they remain unaddressed. The system appears stable because no immediate disruption has occurred, but its structural position deteriorates.

Financial systems require continuous governance because their structure evolves continuously regardless of intervention.

Control is often interpreted as episodic intervention. It is applied when visible problems emerge and withdrawn when conditions appear stable. This episodic model allows misalignment to accumulate between interventions. Deviation develops gradually, often without clear signals, until it reaches a level that produces visible instability. At that point, control is applied in the form of corrective action. The system is adjusted to restore alignment, and control is again withdrawn.

This pattern produces cycles of drift and correction. Between interventions, misalignment accumulates. When intervention occurs, adjustments must be larger and more disruptive because deviation has progressed further. The system oscillates between periods of apparent stability and periods of active correction, without maintaining consistent alignment.

Continuous control operates differently. It does not wait for instability to emerge. It functions within normal conditions, maintaining alignment as the system moves. Variability is observed and interpreted as it occurs. Minor adjustments are applied to keep the system within acceptable bounds. Deviation does not accumulate because it is addressed before it becomes structurally significant.

Control must operate continuously because episodic intervention allows misalignment to accumulate between corrections.

This distinction leads to the structural definition of stability. Stability is not a fixed configuration. It is not a precise balance between income, expenses, liquidity, and exposure. It is a position within a bounded range of acceptable relationships. These bounds define the limits within which the system can operate without instability. Within these bounds, variability is normal and expected. The system moves continuously, but its movement remains contained.

Alignment represents the system's position within these bounds. It is defined by the relationships between capacity and load, liquidity and obligations, exposure and tolerance. As these relationships change, the system's position shifts. Maintaining alignment requires continuously repositioning the system to keep it within acceptable limits.

This repositioning does not eliminate variability. It contains it. Income may fluctuate, but expenses and liquidity are positioned to absorb that fluctuation. Expenses may vary, but income and buffers are structured to maintain capacity. Exposure may change, but it remains within tolerance defined by the system's ability to absorb variation. Stability emerges from this containment of movement, not from the absence of movement.

Stability is maintained through continuous positioning within acceptable system boundaries.

The system operates as a continuous loop integrating multiple mechanisms. Measurement captures the current state of system components. Detection identifies deviations from expected patterns. Thresholds define the boundaries of acceptable variation. Adjustment modifies system configuration to restore alignment. These processes operate in sequence, but they also function as a continuous cycle, with each stage informing the next.

Drift represents the continuous movement of the system. It alters relationships gradually, often without discrete signals. Overreaction introduces instability through excessive responsiveness to short-term variation. Overcorrection produces instability through misaligned scale of adjustment, causing oscillation around the desired position. Misinterpretation distorts decision-making by assigning incorrect meaning to valid signals. Recalibration resets the system's baseline when prior assumptions no longer hold. Regime change reflects structural shifts that invalidate the underlying model of the system.

Each of these mechanisms operates within the same control loop. They are not isolated phenomena. They interact continuously, shaping how the system behaves under normal conditions and under stress. Governance integrates these mechanisms, ensuring that their combined effect maintains alignment rather than producing instability.

All system mechanisms operate continuously as part of a unified governance loop maintaining alignment.

Failure does not require a single disruptive event. It does not depend on unpredictable external conditions. It emerges from accumulated misalignment within the system. When governance is absent or inconsistent, drift progresses without correction. Exposure increases as dependencies and sensitivities accumulate. Liquidity may temporarily absorb the effects of misalignment, masking the underlying structural deterioration. However, this masking effect reduces the system's capacity to respond, compressing the margin available for adjustment.

As misalignment accumulates, the system becomes increasingly sensitive to variation. Small changes that would previously have been absorbed now produce significant effects. The system appears stable until a variation interacts with accumulated exposure. At that point, instability becomes visible. The event is not the cause of failure. It is the condition that reveals the structural weakness created by misalignment.

Failure occurs when continuous governance is lost. Without ongoing observation, evaluation, and adjustment, the system cannot maintain alignment as conditions change. Misalignment accumulates until it exceeds the system's capacity to absorb variation. At that point, stability cannot be restored through incremental adjustment. The system must undergo structural change or experience breakdown.

Instability emerges when continuous governance fails and misalignment is allowed to accumulate.

The system does not operate in discrete intervals. It does not pause between periods of change. Income flows continuously. Expenses are incurred continuously. Liquidity is consumed and replenished continuously. Exposure evolves continuously as relationships shift. Governance must therefore operate with the same continuity. It cannot rely on periodic evaluation or episodic intervention. It must function as an ongoing process that maintains alignment at all times.

Observation provides visibility into system movement. Evaluation interprets that movement within the context of system relationships. Adjustment modifies those relationships to maintain alignment within acceptable bounds. These processes form the foundation of governance. They do not produce stability once. They maintain it continuously.

A financial system remains stable only if it is continuously observed, evaluated, and adjusted.

The Money Stability Series

Money Stability*: How to Build Financial Control in an Unstable World* (Cornerstone Volume)

Liquidity and Runway: *How to Build Financial Time, Extend Your Runway, and Stay Stable in an Unstable Economy*

Income Stability: *How to Build Predictable, Durable, and Resilient Income*

Expense Stability: *How to Control Spending, Reduce Leakage, and Create Consistency*

Risk Stability: *How to Control Exposure, Limit Downside, and Stay Financially Stable*

Financial Decisions: *How to Reduce Mistakes, Limit Risk, and Make Better Decisions Under Uncertainty*

Governance Stability: *How to Maintain Control, Prevent Drift, and Adapt Over Time*

Future titles expand the Money Stability framework:

Financial Stability

Part of a Broader Stability Framework

The Money Stability Series is part of a larger stability ecosystem published by Perennial Publishing.

Related domains include:

Metabolic Stability — biological load, energy, and recovery capacity

Career Stability — income durability, positioning, and transition resilience

Mental Stability — cognitive steadiness under pressure and uncertainty

Emotional Stability — regulatory steadiness in environments that do not slow down

Each domain approaches stability as a structural problem: capacity versus load, buffers versus shocks, and governance versus drift. Together, they form a unified framework for long-horizon durability across the major systems that determine life trajectory.

About Perennial Publishing

Perennial Publishing produces practical systems guides for building stability in an unstable world.

Our books explore the foundations of long-term resilience across health, finance, career, and everyday decision-making. Each title focuses on clear frameworks, durable principles, and practical strategies that help readers build lasting stability rather than short-term fixes.

The Perennial catalog includes series on metabolic health, financial stability, career systems, and personal consistency. While each book stands on its own, they share a common goal: helping individuals create durable systems that support a stable and sustainable life.

Made in the USA
Monee, IL
05 November 2026

67386751R00125